DIYA SETHI graduated ~~from~~ ᴀ 2002 – she lived and worked in both the United Kingdom and India until 2010 – in October 2010 she moved to Sri Lanka and began to write her story. Diya currently lives in New Delhi where she works in the capacity of a freelance consultant chef.

THE ADDICT

A Life Recovered

DIYA SETHI

HarperCollins *Publishers* India

First published in India in 2015 by
HarperCollins *Publishers* India

P-ISBN: 978-93-5136-831-1
E-ISBN: 978-93-5136-832-8

2 4 6 8 10 9 7 5 3 1

HarperCollins *Publishers*
A-75, Sector 57, Noida, Uttar Pradesh 201301, India
1 London Bridge Street, London, SE1 9GF, United Kingdom
Hazelton Lanes, 55 Avenue Road, Suite 2900, Toronto, Ontario M5R 3L2
and 1995 Markham Road, Scarborough, Ontario M1B 5M8, Canada
25 Ryde Road, Pymble, Sydney, NSW 2073, Australia
195 Broadway, New York NY 10007, USA

Typeset in 11/14 Granjon LT Std
by Jojy Philip, New Delhi

Printed and bound at
Thomson Press (India) Ltd.

I dedicate this story to my family — my mother, father and brother from whom I hope to find forgiveness and respect; their forgiveness was never denied me, it was I who could not take it ... Their respect I hope to earn from this writing of my story.

PROLOGUE

'Alas for those that never sing,
But die with all their music in them'
            – Oliver Wendell Holmes

As I put pen to paper, I can feel it again: a fierce pain I was once unable to define – a pain that diseased me, eroded every part of me, a pain I now see mirrored, magnified, distorted or disguised in so many different people ... But I found my own way and I continue to do so each and every day.

This is the story of a child, me, a child who was rejected, ridiculed, hurt and humiliated. And she escaped; she became someone else, I, someone to whom she gave the right to damage, deform and very nearly destroy me – a right that was never mine to give.

I am thirty-nine years old and I never thought I would make it this far. For a long time I never wanted to make it this far, but I did, at the end of a long and treacherous road that brought me back to myself, to who I am and to the life that was meant to be mine.

I met me again at the age of twenty-six – we had been estranged for thirteen years, and after another thirteen years of a life lived beyond my wildest dreams, in which I became my own best friend and guide, I know it is time to tell my story, unrestrained and unadulterated.

I have been told, frequently, that I should write; not become a writer, but just write something. I never really understood the suggestion. I had, at best, written amateur pieces on food and cooking, and a few unpublished restaurant reviews. The former received praise for the human character I brought to food, not a unique style in its genre, but perhaps the mere novelty of my being a somewhat erudite person ignited the soft applause.

The latter were sumptuously devoured for their scathing descriptions and brutal depictions, an even more common, and worse, 'easy' way to win a few laughs. It is insidious how compelling humour is at the expense of someone or something else.

But to really write something? I was confused: if not on food, a subject in which I have some kind of credibility by virtue of being a trained chef in possession of experience, passion and knowledge, then, I asked myself, what could I possibly write on with the very same ingredients?

I am not an imaginative person, to be able to invent a story. Even if I chose to represent reality, I am shy in the matter of romance and the intricate illustration of intimacy, which is what sells such stories. And all that is underpinned by the use of technology is little understood by me – yet another enormous range of ideas rendered inaccessible to my wandering mind. So what could I possibly write on? The answer: my life.

All too abruptly I found my high self-confidence and

low self-esteem go into battle, culminating in the question: who could possibly want to read about my life?

After much deliberation, I answered the question with what I would describe as a retiring, rather than assertive, self-confidence: I found relevance in a candid recitation of twenty-six years of my life to the lives of others. And so I thought, why not? I had all the essential elements, except in this case, the expression of passion has been replaced by raw pain, and my life experiences documented without detachment.

I was sixteen when I realized I was sick. And I was high, so high as I virtually floated down the corridor of my high school that day in the United Arab Emirates. Even the scorching heat could not penetrate the oblivion borne of malignant malnourishment, which I was about to diagnose. Yet again, I hadn't eaten a meal in days, and if I ingested anything at all, it was expelled through a merciless fit of vomiting I induced, until acid bile coated my mouth and corroborated the emptying of my digestive tract.

It was very sudden when it hit, as, I imagine, does a stealth missile, a fear which strangled my mind and crudely extracted me from my cloud into an unwanted reality – I was not high. I was weak, sick, and worse still, I had made myself sick. 'No,' shouted one of the many voices in my head above the incessant chatter as I staggered into sitting position on a chair in an empty classroom, 'no, you didn't do this to yourself.'

I felt possessed, and it was within the fraction of a second that I fleetingly met my other person, the one who had made me sick, the one who had plunged me into an eating disorder known as anorexia-bulimia nervosa.

I was sixteen years old and I was an anorexic – what I didn't know then was that an anorexic is an addict, and an addict can only survive in hiding, in the denial of sickness and on a bed of lies. Much like a fungus, the addict grows and multiplies its forms and manifestations in an isolated environment, both emotionally and physically unhygienic.

It had begun in southern Africa when I first encountered racist segregation and in my hapless efforts to circumvent it, I had fallen victim to savage discrimination. I deluded myself into thinking I would be the exception to the unwritten rule, dismissing any endeavours by the coloured to mingle with the white Africans. But very soon I realized I was not welcome and I was not wanted.

In the little world I inhabited, the kind of world we all define in the attempt to be masters of our lives, I lost control. Gradually I began to develop a new person within myself, one who would live in an imaginary world I dominated, a world in which I became all-powerful over my own body; I assumed illusory control of how much sustenance I denied it, how cruelly I played with it and how severely I injured it – what I didn't predict was that I was giving birth to a monster who would, in turn, punish me.

As I wilted on that chair in the classroom, I realized I had to protect myself from myself; I had to reveal myself to another person. Somewhere in my subconscious, I knew I needed help to expose and exterminate my self-made other. The day I told that person was the day I began my journey of recovery on a road less travelled; it was a road which meandered through a fascinating study of addiction and an examination of the human psyche through my own experience of life. I abandoned all documented theory, lectures and diktats by those professionals who preach avoidance, encourage a separationist lifestyle and ultimately instill fear.

During the course of my recovery, I wrote myself the following note; it was a reminder to keep going and to find my own way:

It is to be mourned, the fact that, today, living is considered a form of art which requires teaching; even worse, it might not be absolutist to say that to ensure its own survival, this kind of instruction encourages human beings to detect, if not actively search for, dissatisfaction with themselves and their lives.

There does exist learning that is not a pupil of teaching – that which does the process of discovery access. Teaching not only pre-empts this but is also limited by the use of an intellectual medium that impairs the functioning of the senses.

The pupil must object, the objection carefully camouflaged as questions to which the answers are generously provided within their own framework: Should the art of living not be derived from the act of living? Is it not a form that shapes itself only in the experience of living?

The pupil will then realize there is something absurd in the measurement of a successful life that relies on an individual's overt declaration of his or her perceived state of being; there is a specific vocabulary used in which there are words such as peace and distress, happiness and misery,

each varying greatly both in explanation and expression –
the declaration itself defines and imprisons, it often instills
the fear of loss of a state of being, or the desperation to attain
another state of being. It does not promote reflection and
self-discovery; it magnifies dissent within oneself.

In semantics alone, the art of life reminds us of the art of
war; I wonder then if life too finds definition in the presence
of an enemy. While the art of war emphasizes the need for us
to know our enemy, the art of living instructs us to find our
enemy, which it guilefully suggests, lies within.

Shakespeare wrote: 'All the world's a stage, and all the
men and women merely players.' Alas, for that to be true,
we, the men and women, must follow a script on a stage we
will find only in our complete devotion to a cause, a religion,
a philosophy or something that denies individual expression
and demands the renunciation of much life experience. It is
this very experience that is essential for the natural evolution
of a form of art and not an imposed one drawn from the
example of a minority of human lives.

In the end, is a life that inspires art not more appealing
than one inspired by art?

But this had already been said, and far more eloquently:

'I shall no longer be instructed by the Yoga Veda or
the Atharva Veda, or the ascetics, or any other doctrine
whatsoever. I shall learn from myself, be a pupil of myself;
I shall get to know myself, the mystery of Siddhartha.' He
looked around as if he were seeing the world for the first
time ...

                                   Herman Hesse, Siddhartha

ONE

But what did I do wrong?

My first memories are cloudy and begin somewhat late, in Peking, China.

Until I began writing this story, I had little curiosity about my life before my first memories. But now those years have been revealed to me and they appear to be the most beautiful ones of my life: I lived each moment in the present, my mind virgin and guided by the senses, a mind in which nothing remained etched. I imagine this is true for everyone, but there must be very few who contemplate the idea and are able, in the course of their lives, to restore that virginity and with it the power of all possibility.

A year before my birth, my father, a career diplomat, was posted in New York City to be a part of the Indian delegation to the United Nations. He and my mother had their first child in 1973 – my brother, older than me by just seventeen months. In 1974 I was born at the Lennox Hill Hospital, a place I revisited in my early twenties on my birthday, August 26, and where I marveled at the babies born that day.

I followed the arrival of my brother into what was

a real shelter, I have been told; one constructed by the complete love and unity of two people, my mother and father, for whom the world outside existed but did not invade. It was a cocoon that remained well into the years I do remember.

I have seen photographs of myself from those first years of my life. I have looked carefully, examining my expressions, searching for some indication of who I was at my origin and perhaps still am at my core. I have seen wide-eyed curiosity and sheer innocence, but something went terribly wrong, and for as long as I can remember, I have asked the question: 'But what did I do wrong?'

As a child it was much more deliberate a question asked with determination, and then it was answered: I lied, that was wrong; I spied, that was wrong; I took without asking, that was wrong; I spoke out of turn, that was wrong; I 'demonstrated' my ignorance – a reprimand favoured by my father – that was wrong, and I was loud, that was wrong. So I set about correcting all that was wrong – some successfully, some not. I stopped lying, I stopped spying, I didn't take without asking, but I did speak out of turn. I was loud and, unwittingly, I continued to make a demonstration of my ignorance.

Yet I was satisfied with what I had achieved and expected it to be enough for me to live a happy and successful life – being a good, honest person, unafraid of being wrong and with the confidence to be high-pitched, a weapon I used as a child to fight for my right to be heard and acknowledged by my mother and father, in equal proportion to my older brother.

But I was wrong. To be good, honest, unafraid and confident is not enough to garner attention, praise and success – especially success, the pursuit of which is so poorly navigated, its achievement even worse mismanaged.

It was late, but not too late, by the time I understood the notion of success and the feeling it generates. For most of my life I believed, first, that success was defined by others, following a theory of supply and demand. Then I became convinced that it was the result of a solitary quest for self-discovery and self-sustainment, the latter practised and preached by so many dedicated to a life of spiritual pursuit. But that life appears to exclude the physical world in which they live and limit the human relationships they have. I have since learned it is neither, and neither is enough without the other.

> *Don't aim at success – the more you aim at it and make it a target, the more you are going to miss it. For success, like happiness, cannot be pursued; it must ensue, and it only does so as the unintended side-effect of one's dedication to a cause greater than oneself or as the by-product of one's surrender to a person other than oneself.*
>
> – Viktor Frankl

It is the life I lived that forced an understanding and my surrender. That surrender was to the belief in a power greater than myself, greater than each one of us, whether you call it God, the force of nature, or something else. It could have happened sooner than it did; perhaps, for me, it wasn't meant to be. But what is meant for me now is to

fulfil a duty to others in a way that I can only hope this
story will illustrate, as I tell it from my memory. It begins
in 1979, when my father was posted to Peking as charge
d'affaires of the Indian embassy.

I was five years old, my brother six; we were the
best of friends, companions to one another, merry and
mischievous. I was always delighted by my brother. He
infused my imagination with riches more precious than
my inherent sense of wonder and curiosity – the kind of
imagination otherwise unnatural to me. I was frightened
by it when I was alone, I was frightened of my inability
to harness it and I was impatient for what I wanted when
I wanted it. Both my fear and impatience, the origins
of which I have now deciphered, are traits that rapidly
inhabited my character – not only did they warp the
quality of my youth but also my evolution to an adult.

In Peking, my brother and I were enrolled in our
first school – not quite a traditional one. It was operated
by the Indian embassy and situated within the grounds
itself. In that school, there existed a sense of community
amongst the children – their parents worked at the
Indian embassy and they lived in neighbouring apartment
blocks – but I felt a subtle exclusion. It was partly due to
my father's position as acting ambassador for a large part
of his tenure, but even more, I now realize, because of the
absence of a certain 'Indianness' in me – both my brother
and I had an unshakeable Western DNA of which I was
then incognizant. Our mother tongue was English, not
Hindi, and our eating habits American, not Indian – two
benign features that characterized us, but which appeared

to cause discomfort in the other children and served to create a faint discord between us and them.

After we left New York, we lived in New Delhi for two years prior to Peking, two years in which my brother and I were in a type of kindergarten. I have asked many questions about who I was during those two years, but there is no precedent to the threat of being different that I first felt in Peking, which might explain why I embarked on a journey doomed for disaster when I would not run a race for fear of losing.

At the belligerent age of six, I was the best athlete in my age group. But when the whistle blew I was paralysed by the possibility of failure, a possibility that appeared so suddenly, the fear of which briefly infiltrated my entire being – the next time, it dropped permanent anchor in me: I refused to do a school examination when I was unsure of the answer to the first question. I knew the rest of the answers, but to my evolving mind, there were only two choices available: zero or 100 per cent.

Both those events warned of the person I was to become, someone with a fanatical fear of failure, disguised as perfectionist fervour. That fear was generated by my extraction from my cocoon into an ever-changing world – the persistent and almost metallic unfamiliarity gradually weathered the encouragement I received to move forward and it chipped away at any nourishment I had to do so.

In my adult life, which I entered with great trepidation and much later than my peers, I have understood that my terror was borne of the feeling of being deprived of a childhood – there had been no constant, no familiar places and faces outside my cocoon in the first five years of my life and for many years to come. The transient nature of that life induced my desperate clinging to a childlike disposition well into my adult years. Seventeen years later, at a treatment centre for addiction, I learned that it was the foundation of my eating disorder, which both in sickness and recovery, directed much of my life and shaped my person.

Just Pretend It Never Happened …

It is in Kuala Lumpur, Malaysia, where I lived between the ages of nine and thirteen, that I am able to identify the awakening of my addiction to an eating disorder. Many years later I discovered it is a predisposition, not a contracted disease – much like a predator, aroused by fear.

Before my father was posted to Malaysia, we returned to New Delhi and I was enrolled in a new school, 'Junior and Tiny Tots'. The tender embrace of the name was in complete contrast to the harsh exposure I felt within the walls of that school. It was populated by children born and brought up in New Delhi; their relationships with each other resembled those between siblings, their parents frequented the company of one another and their nannies were friends and confidantes. I had even less of a sense of belonging there than in China where, at least under the umbrella of the Indian embassy, I was united with a community of children in a country in which each one was a foreigner.

What I felt at my new school was worse than fear. It was a panic that unfolded with the realization that I was altogether different from my peers. That panic was quickly sensed by the others – like most children, they possessed the animal instinct for detecting weakness – and they treated me with contempt.

I tried hard to be the same as them, to understand their frames of reference and to identify with them. But I was unable to succeed, and the injuries to myself, to who I really was, were all the more grievous. Every morning I begged my mother not to send me to school: my cries fell on deaf ears, cries that were soon silenced, but which remained alive for a very long time.

Two years later, we moved to Kuala Lumpur and I was enrolled in another school, my third one in nine years. Yet this was the first one that felt like a real school to me where, as one of a multinational expatriate group of children, I finally felt I belonged.

I was very excited and on my first day, when the bell rang to announce our lunch break, I confidently sauntered towards a group of girls including Katherine, who was assigned to chaperone me. When she saw me approach, she lifted her hand and with a confidence equal to that of my saunter, but far more regal, she waved me away. I was not wanted.

The force of that swift yet thorough rejection and my unconcealable humiliation – for I imagined the whole school was watching – continues to resonate in the pit of my stomach when I recall the incident. It is almost like being in an airplane when there is a sudden drop in altitude …

I blinked and hesitated, as if I myself had changed my mind, and it was in that moment that were erected the first walls of what became my prison of defence – it is unarguable that being defensive imprisons human character and personality, so often camouflaged by, or misunderstood as arrogance.

I turned around and walked towards the school gymnasium as quickly as the formidable weight of humiliation would allow. I had to hide, not only from the rest of the world, but also from myself, that self which had just been rejected. I crouched on the ground and opened my lunch box; inside I found the comfort and security of home: peanut butter and strawberry jam sandwiches.

I ate slowly and deliberately, until I felt a soft application of ointment to my wound, the replenishing of something that had been stripped away. Thus was watered the seed of my eating disorder. But I was to suffer worse embarrassment before I relinquished myself to addiction.

Just pretend it never happened, I told myself, and it helped. Yes, it helped me to face the world, to bury my person and create another and, what is worse, to believe my own lies, a virtual cancer I had to battle repeatedly to expel. But God works in mysterious ways, both his wonders and punishments to perform.

My young body developed prematurely just as I was beginning to raise a new person from the burial ground of my natural self. It was neither a transformation nor a natural evolution, but the dangerous deformity of multiple personalities I was giving birth to.

I quashed all my natural instincts and academic abilities, and tried to distinguish myself in sport, as a faster and more effective way in which to integrate and win over my peers. But I was punished: my chest grew, it heaved and swayed when I ran, played hockey and netball; my midsection widened, suffocated by my leotard, the obligatory uniform in gymnastics class. And as I tried to assume a pretty posture on a balance beam or take a lissome leap in my floor exercise routine, my triumph turned to tragedy. I was teased and mocked, then finally, most punishing of all, I was pitied. There is only one type of pity that is palatable and that is of the self, by the self.

I withdrew further into my life at home, and I found fulfilment in the company and union of my mother and father, especially in the unfailing companionship of my mother. She was blissfully oblivious to my physiological chaos and the umbilical cord I was trying silently, yet frantically, to retie. I was desperate to stifle the loneliness I felt in 'being different' – so feared by the child, celebrated by the parent and coveted by the adult – cruel contradictions that must be negotiated with care and caution.

My family became my everything; it still is.

TWO

*Dear God, please let my mother and father live for ever
and ever and ever, and always be together*

These are the words with which I lulled myself to sleep.
Such was my desperation and fear, not only in my isolation
from the rest of the world but also as witness to the first
crack in the union of my parents.

I remember my father asking me with whom I would
like to live; he had taken for granted that my brother
would remain with my mother. Little did he know of my
furtive efforts to secure an attachment to my mother, and
even less conscious was I of the effortless and unbreakable
bond between mother and son.

I felt a stabbing pain when I answered my father, the
kind of pain that only guilt can inflict. I tried to tutor my
gradually rising hysteria by emphasizing the need for me
to remain with my mother: 'But papa,' I said, 'what will I
do when I get my period? I have to stay with mummy.'

If my father felt hurt and let down, what I suffered
was equally, if not more, chilling. That day I gave myself
a verdict of guilt, generating deep shame and a sentence
of self-loathing in which the words I had spoken to my
father reverberated for a very long time.

In just that brief episode of my life, I encountered guilt, felt shame and began to hate myself. But my parents reunited, and that was enough. To my diseased mind, my own suffering was a necessary sacrifice for the reunion of my mother and father. It was a dangerous interpretation, about to lead me further away from the fine balance imperative to survival and where better could that instinct for survival have been tested than in the racist climes of southern Africa, notably in Zimbabwe, where my father was next posted as Indian ambassador.

And I failed, for survival cannot be substantiated by a living, breathing body, and in hindsight, that is precisely what I would reduce the quality of my life to in Africa.

I had an unfit mind, tortured by concepts it couldn't fully comprehend, and at the age of thirteen I sought to understand what I was feeling in a book entitled *Games People Play* by psychiatrist Eric Berne. It was possibly the most misleading of all the experiments I conducted in trying to help myself. What I grasped from the very title was that the playing of games is not only an inescapable but essential component of human nature, that the end justifies the means – clearly not what Berne intended to convey.

The end to me, in that phase of my life, was to become popular in school and have my parents stay together, both things at any cost. While I don't recall having to bear any expense for the latter, my endeavours in the former came at an enormous cost.

I was seeking popularity through pathological lies told from a vehicle of superiority – I was the daughter of an ambassador and I believed that status alone would protect me from racist jibes towards the Indian and African minority at the prestigious all-girl school in which I was enrolled. I told tales of friendships I had forged outside my school, of boys' attempts to woo me and of ambassadorial parties I was called upon to attend, dutifully and decoratively.

At first the illusions I created and disseminated, like a virus, did bear result: I was invited to parties by the white girls and celebrated in the homes of the Indians and Africans as a virtual VIP guest.

Then one day, it all came crashing down. At an all-white party to which I had been invited, a young boy glanced sideways at me and with a smile that curled at the corners of his mouth, he shouted out loud, 'Long live Union Carbide!' in reference to the infamous disaster of a deadly gas leak from a pesticide plant in Bhopal, India which had killed thousands of people.

I froze. He edged closer, looked me in the eye and said, 'Go home, behenji,' pronounced *bungee* by him, in origin a respectful Hindi word for a lady, but not in its pronunciation by the white man for the Indian woman in Zimbabwe in the mid-1980s. I was not welcome and I was not wanted: the message was clear and the impact deadened my senses. Even today, every time I see a smile that curls – and I do see it on many faces – I cower at its threat to maim.

If I could have cried and felt, profoundly, what I was meant to feel, I would not have done what I did next, the consequences of which were much more harrowing. If I had allowed myself to feel vulnerable instead of shameful, it might have been a turning point in my life. But I was saturated with shame, and that shame gave sustenance to my lies.

I was unable to find sanctuary at home, where my brother had become the priority. I was jealous, yes, I felt betrayed, yes, even if my cries for help were silent screams that could not be heard. Eventually, when the churning of jealousy and betrayal took on a momentum I could not withstand, I reprimanded my mother, and when I did, I learned a valuable lesson which held me in good stead later in my life.

She explained to me that I was simply different to my brother, like chalk is to cheese, and it was I who determined another person's approach and response to me.

Somewhere in my subconscious, I knew I was so deeply buried beneath a damaged façade, I could neither be seen nor heard and the approach and response by others were to someone I pretended to be.

Today I see a virtual graveyard of people around me, so frightened of the unknown that appears when they reveal themselves. They are terrified of baring their vulnerability – misconstrued as weakness – and of the inevitable change in equations that ensues. So they continue to bury themselves in the abuse of mind-altering substances, they abuse their bodies in an attempt to thwart time, and they abuse each other when they are steered by the most powerful drug of all: control. The desire to be or the illusion of being in control surreptitiously destroys not only the quality but also the breadth of life. What they don't know, just as I didn't then, is that above the burial ground shines the bright light of real liberty and limitless possibility, which transcends both mind and body.

It occurred to me that my brother had been wise, true to himself and accepting of circumstance; he had not allowed himself to fall victim to it. He had withdrawn, but not so much as to provoke unwanted attention. Instead, he quietly channelled his energies and he excelled in both academia and individual sport. His achievements won the silent respect of his fellow students and sportsmen as well as the vigorous attention of my parents, which had its merits and faults. But I was far too consumed by self-pity to be able to detect any anxiety in him. I don't know if there was any, except from the consistently high standards set for him by our parents.

My brother has always been a subject of guesswork for me. The only indication I received of his having endured some torment of living in a racist society was a letter he once wrote to me from Winchester College, England. In it, he ended a sentence with the words, 'and no one here has a racist bone in their body …' It was a letter that radiated positive affirmations even without the employment of any emphatic language.

I saw, I read, and I felt relieved in the knowledge that I was in an extraordinary, rather than ordinary circumstance, that this too would pass and that my definitions of the world were vastly limited and flawed

Alas, it was but a momentary revelation, unable to compete with 'the power of my now', my addiction to lying and getting away with it.

The telling of lies was the first manifestation of my addict personality; it knocked me to the ground but not rock bottom, the latter an almost vital prelude to the admission of addiction.

I was like an alcoholic saying 'this is my last drink'. Except I was saying, 'this is the last lie I will ever tell', in my effort to be wanted and needed. But I couldn't stop fabricating my fairy stories of love, laughter and celebration until the day I was stripped not only of my false dignity but also manufactured self-worth.

My alleged friends, comprising both Indian and African girls, announced a gathering on the school grounds to which they invited the rest of the girls in our student year. They then proceeded to expose me lie by lie, weakness by weakness and betrayal by betrayal. They had come well armed, carrying proof of my life, routine and extra-curricular activities, the sources of which were the embassy driver and one of the local staff members at our residence. A girl named Nira was nominated to be spokesperson and she stood tall and erect while she made an exhibition of me before the others.

I quivered as I failed to find my voice to issue denial or defense, and I sat there mute for what felt like an eternity. Gradually I deafened myself to the recital of my lies and deceit as I became immersed in an imaginary world where it was all true.

I was looking down at the ground when I heard Nira call my name. She asked me what I had to say for myself. I raised my head to look at her and without responding, I stood up and walked away, my eyes swollen with unshed tears – I didn't shed those tears for eleven years. Instead, I tried to stop lying and for a while I was successful, but the mind of an addict manipulates the truth; it finds blame and justification for its misdemeanours and, above all, the memory of an addict is short-lived.

In the initial aftermath, there was no such blame or fight with the truth, only flight. I pleaded with my parents to allow me to change school; I never told them why, but they acquiesced in view of my ravaged appearance and battered demeanour.

I had put on a noticeable amount of weight by eating strenuously to suffocate my shame. Even if it was by no means enough to call me fat, it was more than enough for me to resort to controlling the warped world that lay within my mind in the only way I could think of: by starving myself. At the age of fifteen, I became an anorexic.

At first it felt heroic to watch the seconds, the minutes, then the hours roll by without any nourishment. It was like holding my breath underwater, until the panic began. Hunger would strike in the depths of my stomach, a feeling so terrifying without the promise of imminent relief, even in the absence of any physical pain. But contrary to being underwater, where the end comes quickly if you don't come up for air, starvation will torture you, slowly and surgically.

When the feeling of valour vanished at the end of a day, it was replaced by a tidal wave of hunger that crept up slowly from my hollow stomach, to my chest that constricted in fear, then to my throat that tightened in the resolve of denial and finally to the gates of my mind against which the wave would crash and my eyes burst into a flood of tears.

I wept at the self-inflicted punishment of hunger. I wept for release from my captor, until I was swamped by a sense of victory and that duplicitous lightness of being, called a high.

Had I known what it is to be truly hungry and thirsty in the absence of choice, as is the case for so many men, women, children and animals, had I been able to break the definitions of my world then, this would not have been the road I travelled, the road I still look back on in anger and apology. My apology is to myself, to the child born on 26 August 1974, named Diya, a little one full of innocence and showered with love …

But in 1989, on the eve of turning sixteen, that child was no longer innocent. She was shameful and when she found herself in danger of being exposed as an anorexic, she adopted the convenient camouflage of bulimia – she became, what is known as, an anorexic-bulimic.

I ate when I had to, in public; I ate as little as I could for the purpose of my dangerous game of pretend, all the while plotting my escape to the nearest bathroom. I would roughly push two fingers down my throat until I gagged and vomited. And if I sensed anything remaining in my digestive system, I would drink as much tap water as I could to flush it out.

Eventually, when my body got used to this routine of punishment following any nourishment, I no longer had to use my fingers. I would merely bend over and my body would be completely submissive to the purging, to the self-flagellation that induced a kind of levitation where I could neither be harnessed nor harmed.

Very soon bulimia evolved into much more than a front that obscured anorexia; it became my primary purpose – to escape my loneliness by foraging for food and to suffocate my feelings by eating indiscriminately. I didn't taste anything I ate, but I would eat feverishly until I could bear no more and was forced to vomit for physical release from the prison of my reality.

It has not been underlined sufficiently in literature on eating disorders, or by authorities on the subject, that both the denial and purging of nourishment generate a powerful high. It is the same high that desensitizes every addict and it is also the cunning trap of anorexia-bulimia – not the skeletal frame the disease engenders. No one in the throes of the illness is able to see the real shape of their own body. No one in the throes of the illness is ever thin enough, until perhaps on their deathbed, and in most cases, not even then.

THREE

It may not be their country, they do not like the colour,
Yet they will not leave to try to find another.
Made a home for themselves they have, in places rich and green,
While the natives live out there in the wild and unclean.

Above, the first paragraph of an amateur poem I wrote
on the eve of leaving Zimbabwe for Abu Dhabi, where
my father held his next post as Indian ambassador to the
United Arab Emirates.

I had seen some harsh realities of life and human
nature in my years in Africa and I felt ruined. I cried
tears of relief and regret as I looked out of the window of
the airplane, but the only selfless tears I shed were on the
grave of a puppy, just before we left. I didn't want to leave
her behind. I wished to be able to carry that memory and
reminder of her for the others.

My mother had acquired a male Lhasa apso in Sikkim
just before we moved to Malaysia and in Zimbabwe
she adopted a female playmate for him. They had four
offspring, one of which was poisoned to death by a snail
pellet in our vegetable garden. I grieved for months, not
so much for my own loss as for her mother and siblings
whose searching expressions broke my heart.

There was nothing I could do, no comfort I could bring them, not even through the re-assuring facility of language and communication. I was helpless but they were not. They had let go with the help of that mechanism, gifted to all living creatures, which human beings are the least able to operate efficiently – we carry our pain with us, we let it control, define and disease us. I should have understood the inevitability of loss and the reality of how powerless I was but I didn't.

Instead I tried to become a second mother to the little family of dogs; they slept with me, ate with me and travelled with me around the globe. For several years to come, they were my unfailing companions and provided nourishment to my pathological need to feel needed and wanted. There were two males and three females – I loved them dearly and I still do, even though they are long gone and have never been replaced.

I am not a mother and perhaps I never will be, but I think I know what it is to be a mother: to feel what your offspring feel as if they are your own feelings, to protect fiercely, help tirelessly and sense neither sacrifice nor deprivation in the face of their needs and desires. At that time, these was the only selfless qualities I possessed, but I later realized they were selfish at their core.

As the airplane began its descent into Abu Dhabi, I recalled a treasured memory hidden in a pile of unfortunate ones of my time in Africa – meeting Nelson Mandela shortly after his release from prison.

It was my father who took me with him to witness that historic event. My dear father who, aided and abetted by my mother, made sure that my brother and I were given every opportunity, complete protection, the guarantee of a solution to any problem and as much exposure as we could possibly have for as long as I can remember.

We went to Harare airport where, along with hundreds of others, I was given the opportunity to shake Nelson Mandela's hand. The thing about being in the presence of such courage, endurance and greatness is that in that moment, everything seems surmountable and God is not merely a distant idea, a symbol of religious convention, an inaccessible purveyor of miracles and an artificial blanket of security. Somewhere in the recesses of my being, where so much sewage was accumulating, that moment left an imprint which proved to be invaluable.

It was the year 1990 and the first Gulf War had just begun; an interesting time to be in the Middle East, especially in the safe environs of the UAE, an R&R base during the crisis. I was almost sixteen and in my element with a waif-like physique, widely celebrated after Kate Moss had revived the much lauded 'twiggy' frame.

The memory of my misfortunes in Zimbabwe had faded enough for me to wallow in unexpected attention and suddenly I found I could make each one of my lies come true. I was invited to many parties where there were boys waiting to woo me. I basked in the glory of diplomatic life with a dutiful and decorative presence at receptions, national days and other celebrations. I went to the palaces of Sheikhs, where Cristal champagne cascaded down man-made waterfalls and beluga caviar was served in silver buckets. Where international celebrities performed and mingled with the crowd and each female guest received a twenty-four-carat gold necklace as a gesture of appreciation for her attendance.

I revelled in that world where I stood out with my tiny, much admired frame and I believed it was the undoing of my lies, my absolution – a belief that gave more fodder to my fraudulence, albeit briefly for my penance was just about to begin.

The day I realized I was sick, it was my mother I told, the announcement made in one long pernicious sentence that momentarily paralysed her. 'You have been watching too many movies,' she said with a panic so acutely visible I shrank away from her. When she spoke again, she had recovered her composure and, quickly, she devised a plan in which I was an eager participant. I was more than aware of the fragile construct of her plan, but such was my shame at the wound inflicted upon her by my confession, I would have agreed to any proposition or punishment.

Her plan was the classic and most ineffective one, the reflex reaction of any parent faced with a child troubled by such an affliction: therapy, designed primarily for the parent to derive a sense of security from placing their child in the care of a therapist – in my case, a psychiatrist – and in building a meal plan in which the child is partnered, supervised and policed.

My mother, bless her beautiful heart, would have my erstwhile favourite foods waiting on the table when I returned from school. She would eat with me or else simply watch and wait until I finished my food. I was made to eat honey-glazed roast chicken, sautéed chicken livers with linguine, rice and lentils, baked chicory with ham, and many other dishes that once yielded such pleasure but then produced a penetrating pain. I would remain under the watchful eye of my mother for as long as I had to, my metabolism so sluggish that my body was able to wait patiently for the expulsion of its nourishment.

For a while I did try. I made a few visits to the psychiatrist, but he himself peremptorily declared me of sound mind and the therapy unnecessary. It was in my sessions with him that I learned to manipulate the truth, and I discovered that the confident declaration of truth was in fact the most secret hiding place for lies.

I easily admitted to him that I was sick. He asked me what grave circumstances in my past had diseased me in such a way, but in his understanding there were none – there was no physical abuse, no trauma, no harm done to me by my mother, father or brother. I was neither in denial nor under any pretence about what he felt were disproportionate reactions to the events that had wounded me. He searched for sociopathic tendencies and found none, he examined my ability to feel and love and was reassured, he looked for cruelty but it was in vain.

He did not connect the dots; he did not examine my present and my thoughts on the future as carefully as he did the past, a pitiful shortcoming of psychiatric evaluation, as complacent as a psychiatrist's failure is in engaging his patient in a dialogue. If that doctor had spoken to me as a fellow human being, shared something of himself with me, he would have seen, and made me see where I stumbled and how I fell. But he didn't, and with a clean bill of mental health, I returned victorious to the cycle of eating, not eating, trying to withstand the nourishment, purge myself of nourishment – a cycle that generated more lies, shame, then worse lies and greater shame.

So submerged was I in my world, the definitions of which were caving in day by day, there had to be something that would shake and shatter my living slumber. And there it was, something terribly cruel and deservedly so.

FOUR

Dear God, No! Please don't do this to me, please help me

Just as human beings instinctively show impatience with a beggar and wave him away, so does God. The power that is God does not hear begging. Begging is not believing, believing is not needing to beg; it is not the attempt to influence an outcome through the force of a plea.

> *If it's meant for you,*
> *You won't have to beg for it*
> *You will never have to sacrifice your dignity*
> *For your destiny*
>
> Chelsis Porter

It was in the morning, the only time of day when I wore no masks and made a vow to myself, one I renewed every day after my confession to my mother. It was a vow of change and self-improvement I made and broke each one of those days. But my spirits soared with the promise to myself, that deceptive feeling of being powerful over my will and ready for battle – a feeling that would slowly unravel during the day, overturned by the forces of the universe which conspired to show me I was not in control.

I was fighting the wrong battle, the one in which I was meant to surrender.

That morning, I looked at myself in the mirror, bright-eyed, and it was the last time I did so without squinting for the next three years of my life, until I turned twenty.

On my forehead was a tiny protuberant growth, which at first, I mistook for a peculiar pimple. I leaned closer to the mirror and saw that it had a strangely flat surface in a light shade of grey. Although barely discernible by touch, it was loud in its visibility, especially to someone whose identity had been built with the bricks of vanity. If it hadn't, I might not have felt as wild with terror as I did, like a deer caught in the headlights of a car. But in that moment I knew exactly what fate held in store for me, a fate I had attracted, not one that was meant to be mine. I had interfered with the laws of biology and I was about to pay a price for it.

That singular growth multiplied in a matter of days and spotted the entire surface of my face. I used concealer over concealer, face powder over foundation to camouflage them, the same way I camouflaged so many aspects of myself. But they could not be hidden.

By the end of the week, I had witnessed the gradual distortion of a face, my face, which had smiled whilst it hid an expression of shame; that shame was beginning to emerge by force.

The day I went to the dermatologist, I felt as if I was given a death sentence: I had contracted a virus called the human papillomavirus, a strain that spawned contagious flat warts. There was no cure; there was only a superficial procedure designed to cosmetically efface the warts and provide temporary relief while waiting for the virus to self destruct.

I was told, in no uncertain terms, that I had contracted the virus as a result of a highly compromised immune system. Yes, I had effectively done this to myself, shouted that same voice in my head, while the rest of the voices pleaded for help in the recital of a mantra : Please don't do this to me, God, please help me ... But it went unheard.

And so it began, another cycle of self-indulgence, this time motivated by vanity, the burden of supervision and expense borne by my parents. The method of treatment, called Cyrofreeze, employed liquid nitrogen to freeze the warts one at a time, until they dried like parchment paper and fell from the surface of the skin. My face would be covered in welts for a few days after each treatment, and then there was some respite before the warts reared their heads once again.

I began to cower, to hang my head down rather than hold it up, and my posture gradually bent with fatigue, not only from malnourishment but also from the weight of shame I harboured.

There was, and is, far greater suffering in this world, suffering that is not self-inflicted. There are people born with malfunctioning bodies, those whose faces are disfigured and mutilated in wartime, others with crippling afflictions that are truly unfair and unwarranted death sentences – but they soldier on, till the end, with determination, dignity and most importantly, an awareness of a world outside themselves. It was not that I was immune to those realities, I just could not face them. And it felt easier, when in fact it was more painful, for me to remain locked inside my tiny universe.

Then one day, I met a man, a man known to me from television and videos, a man greatly admired by my father. It was a privilege for me to accompany him to a private audience with Muhammad Ali, one of the greatest boxers of all time who had been ravaged by Parkinson's disease.

I almost didn't go that day. Such was my narcissism. My face wore traces of a Cyrofreeze treatment and my body was swollen with water retention, a frequent side effect of anorexia-bulimia. But I did go, and I met a great man, a very great man.

Muhammad Ali was in transit in Abu Dhabi; he was on his way to Iraq to meet Saddam Hussein in an effort to negotiate the release of American hostages. When we entered his hotel suite, he looked up and smiled a smile that danced in his eyes with carefree abandon, illuminating his entire face.

He rose, supporting himself by the armrest of the sofa on which he was sitting. He trembled and then shook, but with neither awkwardness nor self-pity. When he finally stood before us, he was much taller than I had imagined, and not just in height. He stood taller than the celebrity he was, and he held out his hand to shake my father's as if the privilege was all his. He stood taller than his disease, which evoked no theatrics in him, nor did he visibly let it define him. As if to allay any such sentiment from us, he made a joke when my father asked him for his autograph – Ali obliged with a signature almost childlike in its writing, and then he requested the same from my father. A moment later he looked at my father's elegant signature and said, 'But Mr Ambassador, yours is just a scrawl.'

I laughed quietly, my eyes brimming with tears, but they were not tears of pity. They were tears of gratitude for my introduction to a man with an indefatigable spirit. Muhammad Ali was a man who was high, really high. And it was on life, on being alive, on the wave of a sense of purpose and the rendering of a public service. In that moment I wanted to be just like him. But I didn't know how ...

... And so I returned to my life of 'grand designs and petty desires' – a phrase my father used in a different context, in a piece he wrote upon retiring from the Indian foreign service in 1998. He is a man with a wealth of intellect and linguistic talent that is hard to emulate, and in this poignant piece of writing called 'Four Titles', he becomes a man with an impenetrable philosophical depth too. I had not seen it in him before; perhaps I did not understand it then. I do now as I look back and then ahead.

What I understood then was that I could redesign my life and change my desires. My grand design was to get away with it, my petty desire simply to be wanted, to be popular at the cost of my self-respect.

My plan was to change my circumstances by changing geography – the great geographical cure, a grand delusion and petty lie that so many of us believe. I felt confident that a different place, new people and a fresh start would allow me to conquer my reality, a reality known to at least three people, the three most important people in my life. My family was an antidote for my sickness but I was being manipulated by my other person, the one who felt threatened by exposure and my coming closer to understanding why I was sick.

The escape was timed well when my mother, the only person to whom I had bared myself completely, was away in France. I convinced my father I was ready to study in England, as he had desired, but at an American university. I articulated my case well and suggested I leave school, engage a tutor to help me prepare for my SAT, the university entrance exam and then relocate to London.

My father agreed, such was my Cartesian reasoning and eloquence – qualities developed by my other person, the addict, which damaged me then but I have now learned to use to my advantage. By the time my mother returned from France, it was too late to change course. Suddenly I was at the threshold of an unknown world and the very thought aroused sheer terror in me. I could not recall having made the decision myself. I had been played expertly by what I call 'my other', that ruinous force which gained momentum as it assumed command of my judgement and control over my instinct.

All too quickly, I found myself en route to London with a sick body, a sicker mind and a skin disorder which, at the very least, guaranteed a return home for treatment every four to six weeks. For the first and last time in my life, I left home with that subtle threat of regret. After I returned and till date, I have never made such a choice again, one motivated by fear and the need to escape.

FIVE

'A foggy day in London Town had me low, had me down
I viewed the morning with much alarm ...'

The lyrics of a song that, somewhat perversely, serenaded some of the happiest moments in my life while I was nestled in the womb of my family – the same family to whom I owed respite from my clinging presence ... But suddenly those words mirrored what I felt. And in that mirror I had to face myself: a sick and frightened eighteen-year-old child.

I lived on campus at Regent's College, London, in a room I was obliged to share with another student – all the single rooms had been occupied. It was an American college housing both resident and exchange students from the US and there were others who lived off campus. The facilities of the college were shared by an adjoining institution called the European Business School – it was largely constituted by students from different parts of Europe who distinguished themselves by virtue of belonging to a better academic institution and by being European rather than American.

Very quickly, due in large part to the debris from

my years in Africa, I detected the different nuances of discrimination, perhaps more palatable as they were not determined by skin colour but no less menacing and unfair. I recognized discrimination amongst the different nationalities in which the entire history and cultural practices of a people might be ridiculed and summarily dismissed. I observed the prejudices of the materially privileged against those leaning on scholarship education, of the academically superior against their less accomplished peers, and of those able to easily embrace a foreign environment against others that treaded carefully on new ground.

In each category, with the exception of one, I felt an underdog. I was there on a scholarship, not nearly amongst the materially elite, and as much as I had been exposed to England and Europe, I did not have a sense of belonging, neither there nor anywhere else for that matter, and even if I was fascinated by my new surroundings, I observed them from a position of fear. I was, for the first time, on my own two feet.

I could not lean on my citizenship of a country that was equally rich in history and culture to the British and European ones, for I had no roots in India and feeble knowledge and understanding of my own country. All I had was a superficial exposure to the display of nationalism expected of an ambassador and his family.

Later, my father would lament the fact that my brother and I had been deprived of the cement of our own nationality and culture, with which to build secure identities as boards from which we could spring. Today I am able to disagree. I look back without regret and I look ahead with pride at being able to seamlessly integrate with different people in different places.

There is freedom in being unlabelled, in being a John Doe, in being open to interpretation and allowed to interpret leisurely, as a veritable citizen of the world. Yet, when misunderstood and unharnessed, such freedom is damaging.

In my position of fear, from which emanated that familiar panic, I all but calculated the need to create a family for myself and to distinguish myself in academia – the latter more accessible as I found the American system easy to penetrate with the disciplines I had acquired in my earlier British education. The former was where I stumbled and fell in a manner that was very nearly life-threatening.

The first person with whom I attempted to forge a bond was my roommate, an African American female exchange student, a few years older than I was and a very large girl. I am unable to use the word 'fat' without an eruption of guilt. I have always found it unkind, and more often than not, it is used with cruelty and proposed as the defining feature of an individual, something to which I am vehemently opposed.

Yet, with a lopsided hypocrisy and by virtue of both her age and size, I found myself conveniently blending into the role play of mother and child. I presented myself as a lost waif in need of mothering, and I do believe the peculiar duet we performed was of mutual benefit: it caught the attention of some girls who wished to befriend us. They were two

black girls of Nigerian origin and one white American girl,
all three enviably self-assured and composed.

Much to their amusement, which I misunderstood as
mothering, I was indulged as a novice rather than as a
child, and I received a soft introduction to the infidelities
of scholastic life: smoking pot and binge drinking. I had,
until then, enjoyed a healthy exposure to alcohol and I
possessed little knowledge and no experience of marijuana.
I felt a reflexive rejection of such gratification, but I
concealed my reluctance to participate for fear of being
deserted. Instead I feigned enthusiasm and cooperated
with a manufactured energy that served to weaken the
resolve with which I had left home.

After my very first experience, involving the ingestion
of a vast quantity of tequila shots and a hash brownie, I
lost consciousness. Fifteen minutes later I recovered my
senses and found my roommate perched over me, her
eyes glazed by hashish and her cheeks wet with tears of
laughter, both at my condition and the mouth-to-mouth
resuscitation she was poised to provide. Through the haze
of hashish and tequila-induced hilarity, the girls believed
they had lost my pulse.

I felt a violent blow in the face of such indifference
to my well-being and cruel humour inflamed by my
plight ... But they were not being cruel; they were women
accustomed to taking responsibility for themselves. They
were aware of their limits and limitations for which they
neither apologized nor laid false claim to being anything
other than who they were. I was a parasite craving their
care and undivided attention, the denial of which left me

bereft and blaming them for my own choice to participate in their extra-curricular activities. I silently condemned them for being selfish and self-consumed but they were neither; I was, and I was blind to it.

I had no relationship with myself and I could not fathom being responsible for myself; I wanted others to be responsible for me and to be indebted to me. I believed it would help me secure their friendship, if not their respect and loyalty and, in a somewhat villainous manner, that it would enslave them to me.

It backfired; it always did and it always does. I see it all around me today, this crafty game of give and take in which people ingratiate themselves with one another in an effort to bring durability, rather than quality, to a relationship. It is a game that gradually distorts each player's sensibilities towards the others, encourages fraudulence and ultimately ruptures a relationship in a way that is usually irreparable. There is neither any truth nor genuine emotion at stake in that game, a lesson I learned much later in an affair of the heart.

I was starving in every way, and I was without my family to provide me with the nourishment that gave me the will to survive. The only relief I felt was when I was consumed by my pursuit for academic excellence, but it came too easy and cost very little time. I should have known to respect and nurture that talent, to allow my natural ability to help me broaden my intellectual horizon – but I didn't.

So many of us are unable or unwilling to acknowledge our advantages. Instead, we chase dreams that elude us,

especially when they are not meant to be ours. And often we
let the stubborn pursuit of those dreams destroy us, when
all the while the right choice and propensity to generate
the best outcome lie within us from the very start.

I was in desperate pursuit of that which destroys, and
as much as I tried to keep up a pretense of friendship
with my girlfriends, within me was a steep withdrawal
carrying me deeper into my eating disorder until, to my
fright, it was detected. I denied all accusations with a
quivering voice and unconvincing emphasis and the girls
decided to accept my false statement of truth even though
they visibly did not believe what I said. They were kind,
young women, but they had very nearly exposed me and I
knew I had to make an escape

After a fortnight I was scheduled to return to Abu Dhabi
for the holidays. I had been home once for a Cyrofreeze
treatment; I stayed for just two days, in which I managed
to sustain a sunny demeanour before my parents while
I presented them with a dishonest account of my life in
London.

The truth is I was drowning, but floundering to stay
afloat in any manner and at any expense.

SIX

*'I was a stranger in the city, out of town were the people
I knew, I had that feeling of self-pity, what to do, what to
do, what to do ...'*

I returned to London after a few months' holiday in Abu Dhabi, with an acute sense of estrangement from myself. I quote the above words from the song, *'A Foggy Day in London Town'*, as if Ira Gershwin wrote them especially for me – what they really describe is a common human condition, loneliness, which, when masked, serves to deform the self. I did just that. I concealed the sentiments reflected in those words and I gave license to my pursuit of another path of self-deformation.

Loneliness has so many interpretations for which there are myriad solutions. But in my experience, the loneliness of alienation from the self, it's disguise celebrated by others, is the most threatening to the quality of a life.

My loneliness was born when men praised my talkative faults and blamed my silent virtues.

Kahlil Gibran

My first step was to start smoking cigarettes; it not only justified my lone visits to the university pub but also detracted from my solitude. A cigarette gave me a veneer of self-sufficiency while I secretly contemplated the crowd. I hoped to attract the interest of someone, anyone who would befriend me, take care of me, need me. And I did.

I had effectively fled from the girls who first offered me their friendship and they showed no resistance to my retreat. They knew I was troubled and they did not wish to bear the burden of such responsibility. They continued to be friendly from afar, they took pity on me and conserved the secrecy of my condition. I felt grateful for their disposition, whereas I had earlier vilified them. I continued to be in awe of them and their independence even while I craved symbiotic friendships filled with attachment and debt.

I had been unable to find something to offer them. Their independence was strong and silent, without exhibition or rebellion. It was defined first and foremost by their exercise of a duty to themselves: self-reliance, the badge of adulthood we are meant to welcome, wear with pride and from which we should derive dignity. But I was still clutching at a childhood I wanted to fix.

Suddenly I was no longer interested in academic distinction, an unfavourable outcome of my holiday in Abu Dhabi. My brother had come home too, on a mid-term break from Cambridge University, his admission there, a source of great pride for my parents. I tried to compete by announcing that I had received the best grades in my student year, but Regent's College, London was no rival for Trinity College, Cambridge.

My parents did not understand the grade point average system of American university education, and even if they had, Regent's College, London was anything but part of international university aristocracy that included Harvard, Yale, Cambridge, Oxford and the rest of that ilk. Not only was my achievement not applauded, it was barely acknowledged, all intellectual worth effortlessly stripped from me, deficient as I was in self confidence and entirely bankrupt of self respect. But I must not blame them. Validation is important and uplifting, the greed for it detrimental. It dilutes when sought and received in abundance, it destroys when denied.

I had received my due, in being the best in the environment in which I had excelled but, like a child, I wanted more – it was denied and I let it destroy the one thing that gave me some semblance of sanity: my pursuit of academic distinction.

Instead, after my return to London, I dedicated myself to a daily routine that fostered worse self deprecation. Every morning I spent hours trying to recreate myself in front of a mirror; I applied layers of foundation on my diseased face, pale pink blush across my increasingly hollow cheeks and dark black eyeliner to lift my wide brown eyes that were buried in a gaunt face. My skin had less and less respite from the resurgence of warts in between Cyrofreeze treatments, and I became thinner in my new room on campus of which I was the sole occupant. I would hide there, strangle my thoughts and suffocate my feelings in the vicious circle of anorexia-bulimia.

Once I was carefully attired and adorned, I would collect my breakfast from the college cafeteria and return to my room, while the rest of the students remained in the dining hall. I ate alone, and after I had scraped my plate clean and devoured every morsel of food, I would rush to the communal bathroom and vomit copiously until I was cleansed of all nourishment. Light-headed, I would smoke a cigarette to strengthen the giddy feeling that carried me through my classes for the day with what felt like divine detachment. Then it was time to visit the pub where I added a Budweiser to the cigarette with which I carefully completed my facade. I didn't like the taste of beer, but my senses were being extinguished by a mind slowly conquering the rest of my being. And what I did like was my appearance, the image I carried in my mind's eye that I saw translated in the eyes of others. I yearned to be what they wanted me to be.

Eventually I tasted the fruits of my labour: a hand of friendship extended by two boys in their early twenties. One was English, the other Dutch. There was a complicity between them in which I detected a weakness I was unable to interpret. They were attractive and confident young men, but they did not appear to own the strength of independence. They were bound to one another by a need I could not translate and they seemed to be on a hunt, but not of the kind that characterized virile twenty-three-year-old men in search of sexual partners. I would have shied away from that. I had too much to hide and I believed in the sanctity of virginity until marriage. Moreover, at the age of nineteen, I continued to believe in every little girl's fairy tale of falling in love with a knight in shining armour to whom I would finally surrender my body and with whom I could share my soul.

These boys were different. I sensed their attraction to my costume embroidered with a fragile frame and an aloof posture. They did not recoil from me the way others did, the way humans, like animals, often withdraw from their injured peers. I wanted to be bound to them the way they were bound to each other.

They were not in search of popularity, they seemed to have transcended it. They wanted something else, something they felt I could give them and they could give me. At first, their approach was cautious, and I hesitated. We were like gladiators circling one another until each one lay down their sword upon an unspoken understanding of the need for secrecy and a pledge of trust and loyalty. I had no idea what it all meant, but so heady was the feeling of being truly wanted, of forging relationships that promised symbiosis, attachment and debt, I asked no questions and felt no reluctance in entering what I soon discovered to be the dark world of hard drugs, nightclubs and nightmares.

Loneliness, when masked, is indeed a dangerous masquerade; it is in itself an addiction that gives entry to many worlds, both real and imagined, except the one in which we are meant to be. I lost myself so completely and unconsciously for the next one year of my life, it has been hard to extract any coherence from my memory of those twelve months, but the beginning of the end is clear.

I was cradled in the arms of the Dutch boy and I was shivering. My eyes kept rolling back as I tried to focus, dreading my descent from the high induced by an adrenalin pumping combination of ecstasy and cocaine. But I continued to grind my teeth, my mouth moving like that of a goldfish – a depraved sign of ecstasy intoxication which promises prolonged pleasure.

I was in the living room of a house in Notting Hill, dressed in tight black velvet shorts, full-length sheer stockings, platform heels and a flimsy halter top that exposed my concave midriff, the source of much attention from others and therefore pride in myself. Every morning I carefully examined my abdomen to make sure the inward curve of my stomach was intact. My boyish figure allowed me to indulge in much exposure and exhibitionism on the bars and stages of nightclubs where I would dance with abandon, freed from the prison of myself by a cocktail of chemicals.

But at the end of that night, dawn finally broke over a life I had been living in the dark – it broke to the shattering of a bottle against a human skull and a deluge of blood everywhere I looked.

SEVEN

'La Vie En Noir – Life in Black.'

It was a life I lived from dusk to dawn, like a vampire for whom light is toxic – but I had the benefit of drug-induced slumber or speed that made the twelve hours of daylight bearable. For the other twelve hours, I rejoiced in the relief of not having to think, analyse and face the rugged reality of myself. I basked in the joy of togetherness with people I shared a secret with, a connection by conspiracy – yet I had a gnawing feeling of deceit …

That deceit was what kept me safe from an addiction to drugs. I was already a prisoner of my primary addiction and could not be jailed by another – the drugs were my means to an end, they gave me access to a circle of friends who needed me and who I needed. But for the others, the drug-induced high was an end in itself, an escape from their realities, not from themselves. It gave them solace away from fractured families they wished to punish.

I did not share their reality. I was a charlatan and I kept my own secret closely guarded. My escape was from myself, not from others and my solace lay in a family I did not wish to punish. I felt superior to the others who were part of that virtual cult – others, like me, recruited by virtue of their loneliness and desperation to belong. But I was muscular in my protection from an addiction to drugs – as powerful as I was weak against the onslaught of anorexia-bulimia. Again that apparition of control deluded me, its appearance made of glass, easily broken, ushering in excruciating experiences which enfeebled what little faith I had in humanity.

There was no preamble to what was considered an initiation into the cult. The only prerequisite was a stamp of approval for entry by the veritable ringleader, a drug dealer named Michael, purveyor of any and all mind-altering substances.

Michael had recently been released from prison. He was a slight man with the palest skin and whitest eyes I had ever seen, and was treated with a god-like deference, nothing short of sinister. I felt it then and many times again in my life, the wrongful nature of the renunciation of oneself to another person or group of people, and to the directives they issue. It is merely the flip side of the same coin of control: handing it over in order to contain it, something I came to understand much later.

Michael smiled at me, almost lasciviously, and even in the absence of any sexual energy between us, I felt poisoned. He stripped me bare with his eyes – my naivety, innocence, weakness, which I had tricked myself into believing I had smuggled into this new world, a world in which I was about to discover the potency of symbiotic relationships built on debt. My fraudulence was by no means an antidote to the life upon which I was about to embark.

The orientation took place at a nightclub called The Ministry of Sound, at Elephant and Castle in London. It resembled a large warehouse and was dedicated to drug users. They came in hordes, magnetized by the music played at the Ministry, which in turn played with the senses and sensations of minds and bodies altered by different chemicals.

There was a long queue of people outside; they were minimally dressed and they stood patiently, unperturbed by the wait, which allowed for their substance of choice to take effect. Mine, not by choice but obligation, was a tiny white pill called Ecstasy. I took it hesitantly, with that familiar fear of failure that had always incarcerated me. I was afraid of failing myself by failing others. In my subconscious, I knew I was being led astray by my 'other', and I fought hard against letting the pill take effect until I was warned that the consequences of doing so were suicidal.

The boys gathered around me. They began to tell jokes, they made me smile, they made me laugh, they hugged and kissed me gently, protectively and possessively, until I wallowed in the attention I coveted and gave release to the drug struggling to infect my system …

Suddenly the world was in shades of pink, a world full of freedom, equality, love, music and dance. I danced all night, surrounded by friends and friendly strangers, unaware of my origin and unafraid of my destination. I was high, so high, but it wasn't on life. It was on a lie, and the truth was revealed when the drug began to die an inevitable death and when dusk, as it must, turned to dawn.

That first time, I returned to my college with both Samuel, the English boy, and Wendel, the Dutchman. We stayed in Samuel's room where they gave me their shoulders to lean on while the effect of the drug subsided; when it did, it left an emptiness in its wake that devastated me.

They offered me marijuana to ease the withdrawal but I refused their offer. I was frightened and I did not want to take a drug again. I did not want to have to endure the savage end of another high and if I hadn't already been secured by the anaesthetic effects of my eating disorder, I would have become a victim of drug addiction.

But I did not reveal myself – I was terrified the boys would abandon me, that I had failed their expectations of me and destroyed any faith they had in me. I needed them and they needed me to need them.

Suddenly I was overwhelmed by fatigue; I returned to my room and slept right through the day. I did not attend my classes, neither on that day nor many other days that followed. Sam and Wendel refuelled themselves by snorting lines of cocaine, the effects of which carried them through the daylight hours with exaggerated alertness, sensational speed and false courage. I was yet to earn the credentials that would allow me to graduate to that level of drug abuse.

When I woke up after a sleep disturbed by the agonizing sensation of rising and falling with waves at sea, I was all alone. They were not there, no one was there, to tell me it was okay, to forgive me, to help me forget, and I was without the faculties to comfort myself. I was desperate for relief and for punishment; I was desperate to get to that fine line between pleasure and pain that transports one above both, to a place where there is no sensation at all. It was a place I accessed through food, by eating and then vomiting.

I went to the college cafeteria and, indiscriminately, I gathered as much food as I could. I put some on a tray and hid the rest in my handbag and pockets. I returned to my room where I ate with a punishing force, so violent it nearly choked me. Then I went to the bathroom and vomited, gagged, vomited again and again until I could barely lift my head. When I did, it was back, that lightness of being which silenced the noises in my head and decelerated the beating of my tormented heart.

Soon after, Sam and Wendel came to find me, their timing synchronized with the fall of night that hailed another induced journey of synthetic joy, mock friendship and faux freedom. They asked me to buy clothes, shoes, jewellery and anything else that might embellish my sex appeal and help me accessorize them. I had never appraised myself in such a manner but I did as they asked.

I went to Camden Town market where I bought vast quantities of cheap clothes and shoes, ones that resembled fancy dresses, or at least that was how I justified the purchases to myself. The garments barely covered my emaciated body and I could not bring myself to look in the mirror. I felt appeased by others' appreciation, even if it was for someone I hardly recognized any more. But I was still there, beneath those trappings and under my skin; I was always reminded of who I was by my primary addiction, anorexia-bulimia, which, in a way that is unarguably warped, protected me from a far more lethal life.

I could not see that the appreciation by others was maturing into one of a sexual nature. I still felt like a child, and I confused their appreciation with a kind of parental pride when I was promoted to a higher level of drug abuse. I was introduced to cocaine and then crack, their purest forms made available by Michael – for which he was venerated. There was a time when we indulged in the radical abuse of those drugs, when the nights did not end, daylight never came and all boundaries were stretched and broken. But finally, on one of those occasions, the night did end.

We were congregated in a house somewhere in London, a house belonging to one of Michael's clients who was always willing to provide shelter in exchange for drugs. It was the first time I was given LSD, commonly known as acid, a hallucinogenic drug.

I was both uninitiated and unprepared for the impact of the drug and when it struck, I felt an uncontrollable urge to crawl inside myself, to find myself. I began to cut into my left forearm with a kitchen knife, but I was stopped, just in time.

I was hurriedly ushered out of the house by Sam, for fear of Michael's wrath. He took me back to Regent's College where I stayed with him, in his bed, fully dressed and clutching him. He had turned his back to me and even while I continued to hallucinate, ignorant of what I had done wrong, I wouldn't stop apologizing. When he finally spoke, he said, very quietly, that he should be the one to take my virginity.

EIGHT

'Bring me to the surface, give me air to breathe, let me see the sorrow upon my broken dreams'

– Unknown

I never said no; I never said yes, either. I wanted to be forgiven. I needed to feel cherished again and I was prepared to do anything Sam asked me to.

I undressed timidly and nervously. I had never been naked before anyone, neither man nor woman. I lay down next to Sam and shut my eyes. Moments later, I sensed his body over mine … Suddenly his weight felt like a shelter, his warm breath against my cheek billowed a tenderness, then abruptly I felt a piercing pain and it was over. I lay there waiting for another feeling, any feeling, but there was none. There was no pleasure, nor was there any lingering pain. But this time I wasn't high; I hadn't risen above sensation. I had plunged into a reality in which all my senses had been gravely injured, the vacuum barbaric.

I opened my eyes and I saw Sam standing above me wearing an expression that revealed disgust; I understood it as disgust at my instant acquiescence. He spoke to me as if he had done me a favour of which I was undeserving.

He told me to go and clean myself up, to sleep, and he offered to make things right with Michael and preserve my place in their world. Before I left, he explained to me that I had made the perilous mistake of compromising their highs, of violently suspending their celestial journeys with an action that was not only morbid but also a threat to their sovereignty.

I walked, slowly and deliberately, up the stairs to my room on the third floor and as I did, I began to digest what had happened. All at once I was consumed by a feeling of nausea that nearly suffocated me. In a moment I could not recall, I had broken a dream – a promise I made to myself to guard my virginity – one that had brought me a sense of hygiene, all the more precious in my otherwise unsanitary life.

I was an addict, addicted to an eating disorder and to being wanted and needed. I was an addict who had prostituted herself in exchange for preservation in a world that was itself a whore of chemicals. It was a world in which love, laughter, celebration and control were hallucinations – they were counterfeit. But I did not permit any sorrow to rise to the surface. I granted myself another decree of shame.

I wish I could have known then what I do now, that when a dream becomes a standard we set for ourselves, we create boundaries that are precarious and we let their transgression foster self-condemnation that is difficult to surmount. We allow those dreams to define us, and when they are lost, it is too late – we have already given them licence to disfigure us.

A dream is meant to be distant, it is meant to give us hope and freedom from the manacles of our everyday lives.

But I had been chained to my dream just as I was to my childhood, and that day I was disfigured in a manner that menaced not only my life, but also my ability to give and receive love for years to come.

Instead, I became Sam: someone who would build attachment, mould symbiotic relationships in which I accumulated debt and then, suddenly and unexpectedly, bring down the curtain. That day I was both victim and pupil of the potency of such relationships. I was halfway through a play on a stage and I did not know how to get off. I had nowhere to turn unless I went home and no one to turn to unless I spoke the truth.

So I stayed, upon pardon from Michael, for which I continued to be indebted to Sam, until the day I gave myself to Wendel on the promise of becoming boyfriend and girlfriend. I wanted the title of girlfriend. I wanted it to undo what had been done to me by Sam, to give me the guarantee of commitment and continuity, with or without love, whether or not I reciprocated it. And I did not. I had surrendered my body but I was not going to share my soul.

Wendel was an instrument I used to incapacitate the relationship I had with Sam, to repossess my dignity and reclaim control. I wanted an exit and Wendel was my strategy. He was kind and weak, weaker than I was. But he came from a very prominent family, one that neither Michael nor Sam, would have dared cross by bringing any harm to him. Wendel loved me, he wanted to marry

me, but I did not, could not, believe him. I was much too
scarred by then, and I was as blinded by finding a way out
as I had been by finding a way in.

Until I did, I secured my place in Wendel's life. I
nourished his declaration of love for me and I managed
to seal his attachment to me. There were nights when I
pretended to take drugs. I would spit out the pills when
no one was looking and I manipulated Wendel the same
way the music did. I would lift his high, dance for him,
caress him, bring him water to drink, towels to wipe the
sweat from his brow. I would do anything to stimulate his
dependence on me, as much as on the drug.

My 'other' had taught me a new game, an adult game
of manipulation in human relationships that went beyond
simple lies – a game which cultivated the feeling of control:
a feeling that can never be fully harvested.

It was my reflex reaction to being wrestled away from
my childhood. I had not been able to do it on my own; it
was done to me by Sam with a ferocity that forced me to
mature, in any way, shape or form.

The only form I knew how to structure was one that
swayed from extreme generosity to brutish denial. For
a long time my relationships with men mimicked my
relationship with food. I would give love abundantly,
pretend to receive it graciously, and then deny both with
a malevolence that injured the other and left me feeling
victorious. Wendel was the first person I injured in such a
way – I hurt myself too, for he had loved me, and I, him.

I punctuated my relationship with Wendel, and the
life that had brought us together, the same night Michael

broke a glass bottle on the head of one of our fellow students, a boy named Derek.

Derek had been working for Michael, selling drugs to earn some extra money. One day, Michael detected a discrepancy between the inventory and accounts, and all hell broke loose. I had not been able to escape intoxication that day, but even through my desensitized condition, somewhere in the distance, I heard raised voices and a cry for forgiveness. The answer to Derek's cry had been the shattering of a bottle against his skull.

The impact threw him to the ground and I could see his bleeding head and torso, which had fallen through the kitchen door, the rest of him hidden by a wall. I tried to get up and go to him, but I was held back by Wendel and Sam.

Michael had also punched Derek in the face; his eyes and mouth were badly bruised and he was barely coherent as he continued to beg for forgiveness. Each time he did, Michael kicked him violently in the ribs and I began to scream. Suddenly I felt a hand cover my mouth and I was lifted and carried down the stairs. I was told to wait until a taxi arrived, and when it did, I was hustled inside it with Derek; he had been carefully manoeuvred out of the house and onto the street. I was given instructions to take Derek back to Regent's college and nurse him in my room until the others returned.

All the way back, Derek kept mumbling, 'It's all right, everything will be okay.' He was trying to reassure me, even through his own pain, which he felt he deserved. Derek believed in his complete subjugation to Michael, from whom he did not question any punishment or prize.

I was holding his hand covered in blood from his face and head, but I could not look at him. I recoiled from him the way others had from me, from a weakness in which I saw my reflection. I recoiled from the life we had in common, from my 'other', the addict who had brought me this far, the one who was keeping me sick, the one who was nourished by delusions of being in control. That night I uncovered the identity of my other, the hurt child who haunted me, the child I had to exorcise from my being.

I remember that night as one which marked the beginning of a war, the one I was meant to wage. I lost many battles, but in the end, through voluntary surrender, I emerged victorious. Several years later I read the following words of wisdom by a spiritual guide:

> *Attachments always have something to teach you. They are a debt of learning, which is why it's important to look at them face-to-face until you can understand why you want to hold on to what is bad. You have a 'hot potato' in your hand that's burning you, but you don't want to let go of it. If you literally had a hot potato in your hand, you would simply drop it, so why aren't you letting go of this attachment? You are unable to let it go because you believe that if you do so, your life will be over. This is the basic illusion that keeps us stuck in the vicious circle of sadomasochism. Your life will not end if you let go of this hot potato. You are not this stubborn self-will, pride or fear. You are not this child who you are identified with, who was once humiliated, abandoned, excluded and rejected.*
>
> – Sri Prem Baba

NINE

And I did. I told the truth without embellishment, which might have given me justification, and without illustration, which would have allowed me to lay blame. I went home and I told the truth. I told my parents I had been taking drugs, that my grades had suffered as a result, that it would not happen again and that I wanted to come home. I admitted defeat, and for the first time in my life, I took responsibility for it.

It was liberating; it gave me strength and irrevocably dented the vast reserve of shame and fear I carried, even if it was a shallow dent. I had a long way to go and I was fortunate that I didn't know then just how long the journey was.

When I looked back later, I realized why I had to endure those years in London; why they were an essential part of my recovery. I had to plunge deeper into the world of addiction, witness many of its causes and some of its consequences; I needed to study it, understand it and learn to overpower its various manifestations within me. But at that time, the triumph over my withdrawal from the life I had been living was gradually eroded by my battle with my eating disorder in which I was a weak contender.

I was trying to fight the consequence, not the cause. I was trying to fight the hurt child who haunted me. I did not stop to consider that I was not meant to fight her; she had suffered enough.

While I was at home in Abu Dhabi, my father received news of his next posting, as ambassador to France. He was to leave in six months and it was agreed that I would return to Regent's College for a final semester. Later, I was to join him and my mother in Paris and complete my studies at the American University there. They had said nothing to me after my brave announcement in which I confessed my errant ways and drug abuse. But their silence divulged defeat and, in that quiet, I had heard the crumbling of their respect for me.

During my three month summer hiatus in Abu Dhabi, I fought and lost my first real battle with my eating disorder. I ate sparingly but I tried to retain what I ate, and I found myself temporary employment as a private assistant to an executive of a company called Nalco. I had hoped that my day at the office would serve as confinement against my eating disorder, that it would help me kill the hours in which I was accustomed to killing myself and my feelings. I tried to recover my health and the respect of my parents, but to no avail. I had hidden myself in a cardboard box where I was trying to control my circumstances and sickness through sheer discipline.

That very control revitalized the energy of my other

and she decimated the cardboard box in which I was seeking refuge. I left the job prematurely and regressed into an even more dynamic sequence of anorexia-bulimia: of eating, not eating, eating and vomiting, and there were more lies, more shame, worse lies and even more shame.

The virus that colonized my skin gained equal momentum, forcing me to increase the frequency of the Cyrofreeze treatments. They left my face almost permanently welted during the holidays and kept me behind closed doors until it was time for my return to London.

Once more I was a stranger in the city, but this time I felt no self-pity. Many of the students that formed part of Michael's coterie had been expelled after the incident in which Derek was hurt. Derek himself had moved back home to the Philippines and Wendel was living in an apartment off-campus. I cannot remember what happened to Sam, but I did see him many years later at a bar in London. He was the same: an insecure, frightened young man driven by reckless anger and steered by his ego and blind ambition. Sam continued to trample on everything in his way. We had little to say to each other and I walked away unscathed, even if not de-scarred of my experience of knowing him. I never saw Wendel again, but I have since communicated with him on email and Facebook; he fought his own battles from which he too emerged a winner, not just a survivor.

I had been shown leniency by the dean of Regent's College prior to my return to Abu Dhabi; he had agreed to give me another chance based on the academic promise I had displayed in the early days under his tutelage. I remember feeling grateful for someone, apart from the members of my family, who accepted and forgave me in the face of such shameful truth.

It was that gratitude which helped free me from loneliness and embrace solitude for the remainder of my time at Regent's College. I dedicated the solitude to my studies and retrieval of my scholarship, which had been withdrawn as a result of poor grades. And I did redeem myself academically, but I can lay no claim to courage or determination. I was still an addict, an anorexic-bulimic, and it was my addiction that helped me bear the prolonged period of solitude.

I cleverly devised a routine that married punishment and reward: I would spend my days studying rigorously, without any distraction. I did not stop for nourishment nor rise from the desk that faced a blank wall in my room. I starved and studied until the clock struck 6 p.m., and when it did, I ate and drank as much food and beer as I could, followed by the discharge of both. Each time I vomited it was with greater strength and colossal contempt for myself.

Alcohol allowed me an exit from my own company when it became stifling. I would go to the pub and chat with the bartender over a few drinks, in particular Budweiser, which I had learned to enjoy. The effect hit my nutrient-free blood stream with a force that dazed and confused the hours until I could eat again, until I could vomit again, until I needed to study again.

In an almost serpentine way, the abuse of alcohol crept into my life and inside my system, where it remained long into my years of recovery from the eating disorder. It is the most insidious of all mind-altering substances, the difference between its abuse and addiction coloured in many shades of grey, its social acceptability a toxic fuel that permits easy concealment and even easier denial.

When I arrived in Paris, I was a bulimic in the first stages of a cross-addiction to alcohol and I had a body that was not only suffering but had also begun to reveal its persecution. My malnourishment was betrayed by a distended abdomen, my face was swollen from water retention, my teeth were full of cavities and the enamel had worn thin from the acid reflux produced by vomiting. I had an oesophagus infected by a fungal overgrowth called candidiasis, and the Cyrofreeze treatments had stopped working; the virus had become immune to my weapon of choice.

I had to put up another fight, but it was motivated by so much fear and despair that I could not have hoped to sustain, or win it without a miracle.

TEN

God works in mysterious ways his wonders to perform.

I was twenty years old; I should have been in the prime of my life, but I was standing at the edge of a cliff and I wanted to jump. I wanted to die, and I felt like a coward for wanting to and not being able to. My body, the only thing in my life that I had thought I was in control of, was breaking down before my eyes, beneath my costume and under my skin.

I wasn't even thin, or perhaps under that swollen mass I was but I could not see it. I would will myself to not look into the mirror until I couldn't bear the denial. Then I would stare at myself from every angle, searching for some kind of redemption; but there was none. My eyes would tire and my head throb with an ache so acute, I was once again separated from my reality.

Overnight my body underwent acute inflammation from the relentless punishment I had inflicted on it, from wounds that were wide open and damp with acid bile in which fungus was breeding. I could not swallow; when I tried, the pain was akin to having a fish bone lodged in my throat. My mother took me to a doctor who, after giving me

66

a superficial examination, called for an endoscopy, the first of many I would have over the next six years. I didn't know what it was. I was told the discomfort was minor and the procedure would be over in the blink of an eye; so I didn't ask for an anaesthetic and wasn't given one.

It turned out to be one of the longest, most arduous minutes of my life. A long tube was placed in my mouth and slowly propelled down my throat until I felt I was being choked. I couldn't breathe through my nose. I forgot how to, and my eyes bulged from their sockets, catapulting a pain right across my forehead. I caught the doctor's free hand and pulled. I gagged as I tried to beg him to stop, but he wore a determined expression, one of complete detachment from my condition as he continued to drive the tube into my oesophagus.

Fifty seconds later, a time immeasurable for the magnitude of pain and terror it yielded, the procedure was over. But the distress instilled a kind of post-traumatic syndrome in me. I felt betrayed and violated, by both my mother and the doctor, a feeling that lasted several weeks. I was diagnosed with oesophageal candidiasis – a fungal infection which occurs in conditions of compromised immunity – and I was prescribed a twelve-week course of an anti-fungal medication called Fluconazole.

In the recesses of my misshapen mind, I promised myself I would never blindly trust anyone again, that I would help myself once the infection was cured – a promise every addict makes each and every day of their lives, the same promise every addict breaks each and every day of their lives.

The infection was contained but I was unable to help myself. Every day in the mirror I saw a face contaminated by a virus which had become immune to treatment, and I gave up my will to fight. I wanted to die and I no longer begged for help in my prayers. Instead, I begged for my end, I begged God to take me.

In my early days in Paris, I was forced to spend a lot of time alone. My mother and father had busy social lives and I would live my days in a trance, hypnotized by defeat and my wish to die.

I made no attempt to make friends at the American University. I would paint my skin with make-up and veil my face as best as I could before attending my classes. I kept my head buried in books I neither saw nor read. They were merely a cover for my polluted being that was withdrawing from life.

I was oblivious to the desperation I had generated in my mother and her ruthless quest to find help for me. She had become my life-support machine, my father the current that sustained her. Every day my mother contacted new doctors, dermatologists, anyone who could possibly help find a cure for the virus while I attended my classes or wandered the streets of Paris.

I sat in cafes and bars where I ate and drank and then I vomited in public toilets. On my way home I would stop at a grocery store and buy beer and junk food to help me survive my evenings alone. After I had eaten my dinner under supervision, I sat with our little family of dogs in the television room and waited for my parents to leave. Then I unwrapped the hidden groceries and ate and drank with a bloodthirsty force to asphyxiate my pain; when I couldn't withstand any more, I vomited continuously until all that remained was the alcohol intoxicating my blood stream, which amplified the high from my discharge.

But when that high dissolved, as it always did, I was wracked with tears, shed onto the fragile shoulders of the dogs. I would tell them repeatedly how much I loved them and didn't want to leave them but that I had to. They clawed at me, licking my face, trying to wipe my tears away, their love unconditional and without judgement. I no longer received that kind of love from my mother.

What I did not understand then was that she had no choice but to deaden her own feelings and become as clinical as that doctor had been, in her unwavering resolve to help me survive. And she did; she gave me survival, but in the end I had to give myself life.

The next hurdle for me to cross was my diseased mouth. All my teeth were ridden with cavities and some required root canal work. I agreed to go to the dentist only when I had to stop eating because it hurt too much to chew. The anorexic in me was happy with the affliction, the bulimic starved of her addiction, but I had given up my fight and I let my mother charter the course of battle.

I did not respond to repeated anaesthetic injections in my mouth and I was forced to endure the crippling pain of root canal procedures. But I had become immune to punishment; I received it as though it was deserved and I let it reinforce my will to die. My mother didn't. She began to fight me as much as she fought my sickness, an expression of love that was in itself an addiction. She became addicted to policing me and uncovering my lies, an addiction as debilitating as mine for both of us.

I felt humiliated and she felt helpless in the absence of a solution, in the loss of control, the most venomous drug of all. Yes, I, like many other addicts, had dragged my mother, father and brother into my world — much later, they too needed help in extracting themselves from it.

In the meanwhile, my mother continued to fight for me and she persevered in her search for a treatment for my skin disorder. She tried a lemon juice cure that burnt the top layer of my epidermis, highlighting the surface of the warts. It took two weeks for it to return to its familiar deformed state, two weeks in which I felt increasingly persecuted by promises of a cure that remained unfulfilled.

I went to the French countryside where my mother had heard of a naturally growing plant, not unlike aloe vera — it contained a viscous liquid, allegedly a cure for flat warts. For over a month, I diligently observed the ritual of applying the gelatinous liquid to my skin each night, only to wake up every morning to a brutally battered hope for recovery. The virus was unrelenting.

Then one day, I found myself on a flight to New Delhi with my mother. She had heard of a possible cure for the virus by homeopathic treatment. I visited the homeopath and allowed him to question and examine me. I accepted his treatment with desperation and disbelief, a duality that nourishes internal conflict and certifies failure. I discovered, the hard way, that life is not a magnet: opposites do not attract the desired outcome, they repel it.

The homeopathic treatment never did work, but in that search I was thrown a lifeline.

On the return flight to Paris, my mother and I forged a friendship with the head steward of the first-class cabin, a middle-aged man named Sunil Chakraborty. He had a magnificent pair of light grey eyes, set in a face that held a soulful expression radiating kindness.

A few months later, he came to visit us at our residence in Paris. I was lying on my bed in fetal position, without any motion or emotion, when my mother knocked on my door and pleaded with me to come down to the living room to greet Mr Chakraborty. It had been eight weeks since I started the homeopathic treatment and there had been no change. The daily agony of hope and disappointment had drained my spirit and carried me into a void in which there was neither desperation nor disbelief, no hope nor faith. I had surrendered myself to a damaged life and when I greeted Mr Chakraborty, it was without the habitual mask I wore or the masquerade I performed.

I sat down in the living room and he asked me if I had ever heard of the spiritual practice of reiki. 'No,' I answered, without curiosity or cynicism. He hesitated, as if to gauge my receptivity to what he was about to say, and then proceeded. He explained that it was a type of energy healing he would like to perform on me. I simply nodded my agreement. He asked me to shut my eyes and I did.

I don't know what happened next, but fifteen minutes later I opened my eyes to see Mr Chakraborty slumped in his chair, his forehead wet with sweat, his left arm stretched

outwards with the palm of his hand pointing towards me. I
felt weak and so did he. I watched him as he slowly opened
his eyes and then, very carefully and meticulously, he gave
me the following instructions: for the next seven days I was
to pour myself a full glass of water every night. Before I
went to sleep, I had to drink half the water in the glass, shut
my eyes and tell myself that my problem would go away.
The next morning I was to repeat the process with the
remaining water. I was to do this for the next seven days, he
said, and with those words, Mr Chakraborty took his leave
and promised to visit us again on his next layover in Paris.

For the next seven days I followed his instructions; I
followed them without desperation or disbelief, without
hope or faith. Precisely one week later, the virus self-
destructed and the warts began to disappear just as
suddenly as they had appeared three years earlier. Within
twenty-one days, there was no trace left of the virus, no
proof of its life nor detritus from its death. Forty-five days
later, Mr Chakraborty came to visit us again, and on the
palm of his left hand, he had one flat wart.

Yes, God works in mysterious ways his wonders to
perform, and even more mysterious are his messengers
through whom they are performed. All that was needed
was my surrender.

I did not see Mr Chakraborty again, until May 2014
when I finished writing my story. I revere his brief passage
across my life and I did not wish to imprison him by my
gratitude.

In May 2014 I went to Bombay to visit Mr Chakraborty,
to lay down my head and rest awhile.

ELEVEN

'No memory of having starred atones for later disregard,
or keeps the end from being hard'
— Robert Frost

I had been given a new lease on life, the terms of tenancy
to be determined by me. But I failed to remember prior
misfortune, and as I graduated from the poor quality
of my former habitation, I celebrated my improved
circumstances with exaggerated vigour that further
weakened my vitality.

I did not understand the power of addiction — the
cunning characteristics which diseased me. I had become
like any other addict or psychopath who begins to suffer
from a poverty of emotion and loses the capacity for real
love and any kind of attachment. I did not realize how
deeply embedded I was in addiction, how far I had been
led astray by my other, that hurt child unable to shed the
memory of her pain or make peace with it. Instead, I
began to run away from myself, faster than ever before,
and the events that took place aided and abetted my flight
until I hurt my wings and fell to the ground.

I was prescribed Prozac by the family physician. We —

my mother, the doctor and I – believed I was suffering from a form of depression, which not only gave birth to my eating disorder but also sustained it. Prozac, one of the trade names for the drug Fluoxetine, is purportedly effective in the treatment of obsessive compulsive disorders and bulimia nervosa. I was prescribed the drug with complete disregard for its possible side effects, which remained unquestioned and unexamined until, eventually, they constricted the quality of my life.

For a short while, however, the drug generated a false sense of happiness that erased any and all memory of my provenance. My mother herself was so profoundly implicated in assuring my survival that she too was blind to the absence of rationale in the diagnosis and treatment.

Very quickly the drug yielded a state of euphoria and an energy that can only be described as hyperactive. I felt greedy for the time I had lost, time I could not retrieve, but I wanted to lay claim to what I could have been. I didn't stop to consider who I was in the present, where I had come from and how best to approach the future. Instead, I regressed.

My vanity had been restored and once I found myself in possession of that drug-induced sense of confidence, I wanted friends, popularity and success, all over again. The drug also served to weaken my appetite, returning me to the less threatening terrain of anorexia nervosa. I began to follow a regimented diet of boiled peas and carrots tossed in a teaspoon of olive oil, a small quantity of which I would consume three times a day.

I ate one pea at a time, followed by a piece of carrot,

and I chewed each one into a puree before I swallowed. I tried to eat as much as would give me nourishment but not make me feel full, a feeling which might have forced the expulsion of that nourishment. I had to calculate how much was enough – neither too little nor too much for me to withstand psychologically.

I could not, would not, allow myself to increase in size, to grow into a woman just as I had into an adolescent all those years ago in Kuala Lumpur; the nightmare of ridicule was raw and robust.

I was frightened of losing the childhood I hadn't lived, to which I kept secure my lifeline, constituted by my mother and father. Through many pleas, with undertones of blackmail, I made my mother agree to my diet. It was devoid of any real nourishment but I promised to regulate it over time. I spent the same amount of time eating as I had in bingeing and vomiting; it was but a substitute, not a real solution. I was submerged in control – in the exercise of power over my will to eat a measured quantity of food – until it was robbed from me.

The new formula I devised was not conducive to a healthy social life of breaking bread with my peers. I began to forge friendships in which the sharing and abuse of alcohol was the common denominator and, as things turned out, it was alcohol that restored the vicious circle of anorexia-bulimia. The effects of alcohol abuse proved to be an antibiotic to the control and concealment of my eating disorder, and its ingestion in conjunction with Prozac had consequences that were menacing.

I befriended the Scandinavian students that sparsely

populated the university, but reigned supreme over the university bar. I would meet them there after my lectures, few of which held my interest. I had stumbled into a Bachelor of Arts degree in business administration with little consideration for how I wished to shape my future and even less respect for my academic ability. One of my electives was business law, for which I seemed to have a natural talent. I remember my professor almost pleading with me to pursue studies in law, but the very notion of commitment was alien to me, my mind and body having been schooled, since the age of fifteen, to respond only to instant gratification.

I lived in the moment, defined by my addictions. The only plans I made were to nourish or conceal those addictions. I lived within the boundaries I could control, as is the case for most addicts, and others, who suffer from amnesia of their past and thoughtlessness for their future.

The power of now can be both slayer and savior – of me, it was a slayer. I had been Scotch-taped together with temporarily repaired teeth, a face to which a flawless complexion had been restored and a body finding an emaciated form again from the retention of a bare minimum amount of nourishment. I had been in a time warp during which I had addressed and overcome the superficial consequences of my sickness, ignoring the cause which, like a bacteria, lay low and dormant until I made myself vulnerable to it again … And I did, again and again, through lies, pretences, a mind-altering drug, an eating disorder and alcohol.

The power of my now was my awakening to the fact that I was living a privileged life in one of the most glamorous cities in the world, at what was meant to be the prime of my life. And I had just been awarded the right ingredients for it. I had grown, by default, into an attractive girl, or at least, that was what I saw in other people's eyes. I had a mass of jet-black hair that fell just beneath my shoulders, dark brown almond-shaped eyes, long eyelashes, thick eyebrows, a dusky complexion, a wide mouth with plump pink lips and a somewhat awkward nose but one that added character to my appearance. I was petite, five feet and five inches in height, with a tiny frame, an athletic gait and a new-found demeanour generated by the prescription drug: it made me bold, boyish and brazen.

I was the daughter of the Indian ambassador to Paris, living in a palatial home situated alongside the Eiffel Tower. It was a four-storey establishment, an *Hotel Particulier*. It was the type of house occupied by aristocrats in the seventeenth and eighteenth centuries. My university, the American University of Paris, scattered amongst various buildings and annexes both old and new, was a short walk away, across the beautiful park that skirted the Eiffel Tower – it is called 'le Champ de Mars', the field of Mars; a tribute to the Roman god of war.

Between my home and university I lived two brilliant lives, an illusion I established for the world around me but not one that I believed in the graves of my mind and soul, where I hid my secrets and where the truth roamed free. I fabricated new personalities to support the illusion, becoming more distant from myself than I had ever been while trying to find the nourishment my ego craved.

At university, I was especially attractive to the blonde-haired, blue-eyed Vikings with whom I developed a bond built solely on the foundation of alcohol abuse. I had nothing else in common with them. They had never travelled outside Europe, and I had a nationality and lifestyle that were entirely foreign to them, except to one young man from Finland named Karl, a veteran traveller who had visited India on numerous occasions. He was about five years older than me, from a well-to-do family in Finland, and he had decided to acquire a university degree after sowing his wild oats.

Karl was fascinated by me and my life. It was a life I had been sleepwalking through until his profound interest in me made me recognize my privileges, none of which I had truly exploited. Karl, like other men, became fuel for my self-confidence. I would wilfully attract men upon the slightest expression of their interest in me and I would toy with them, just as I had with Wendel. I took that gamble until the warning signs of attachment manifested, and then I withdrew without explanation, but with a brutality that appeared sinister. It wasn't. I just could not and would not allow anyone to do to me again what Sam had done. So I abandoned ship before it could abandon me.

There are very few men with whom I shared an intimacy, willing to have anything to do with me today, even when I have tried to make amends. I have faced their wrath, and I have had to forgive myself in the absence of any forgiveness from them; the latter, perhaps, too easy a way out.

At first Karl and I were just good friends. He was already in a relationship with a girl, but she did not like to partner him in his favourite hobby: drinking. He was a heavy drinker with a high tolerance for alcohol, and I would drink with him, ignorant of the effects of alcohol abuse. Previously, my consumption of alcohol had served merely as an accessory to my primary addiction, but it was fast becoming an equal.

I would make sure to sober myself up before I went home; once again, I was being included in all the glamorous aspects of a life that was part and parcel of my father's position as Indian ambassador. My mother was forever watchful, her fears for my well-being allayed only by my proximity to her. I was careful to not mix my two worlds, for fear of being exposed and I tried to restrict my friendships to men, preferably older ones, to whom I imagined I was less transparent.

Women frightened me; I had neither recovered from the rejection by that little girl in Malaysia, nor from the public humiliation by my girlfriends in Africa, and I shuddered at the memory of my near-exposure by the girls I had first befriended at my university in London.

I had never identified the true source of my wounds nor understood them, even as I approached the twenty-first year of my life. Instead I became intoxicated by the exposure I received, an education in itself, but one that was premature for me – I was an emotionally handicapped child wearing the costume of an adult, with a mind that effortlessly adopted all that would make me appear mature and intelligent, but none of it did, I ever truly assimilate.

I learned the art of conversation and how to conduct myself in the drawing rooms of aristocrats and diplomats, the rich and the famous. I attended private dinner parties at the Chateau de Versailles and cocktail parties at the residence of Pamela Harriman, then American ambassador to France and a personality in her own right. I went to the Cannes Film Festival where I dined at the table of the president of the festival alongside Angelica Huston and Francis Ford Coppola. I maintained a studied, quiet demeanour when I wished to pique the interest of others, or else I affected a voluble vivacity if I was sure of being appreciated.

During my father's tenure as Indian Ambassador to France, I also attended the French National Day celebrations at the Élysée where I was introduced to two consecutive presidents, Francois Mitterrand and Jacques Chirac. I spoke some French, largely as a result of my parents' proficiency in the language, but I did not speak it as well as I could have. As with everything else, I learned just enough to trick my way into earning the respect and admiration of those I met.

I watched closely as my parents received many a VIP at our own residence – or rather, the residence of the Indian ambassador. They hosted a party to launch a perfume by Jean-Louis Scherrer called 'Les Nuits Indiennes', Indian nights, and I was asked to model a Scherrer gown for a magazine as a tribute to the perfume. Sometime later I received a request to model a gown for Gianfranco Ferre, one of a series designed as an ode to India and to the Indian sari. It was his last collection for the house of

Christian Dior, where he was the head designer in the mid-1990s.

My ego was nourished beyond my wildest dreams, and I found myself increasingly solicited by young aristocrats, authors, publishers, movie directors and many others. I dined in my own home with Ismail Merchant and James Ivory; they were filming *Jefferson in Paris,* and they brought to dinner their entire cast including Greta Scacchi, Nick Nolte and the then little known Gwyneth Paltrow. I observed everyone and everything carefully – the personalities and roles, the sincerity and duality, the strengths, vulnerabilities and the invisible currents that united or divided human beings – and I learned to ingratiate myself with each person on every occasion.

But I was an impersonator. I was never truly present, and I presented myself to the world in an attire that felt uncomfortable against my skin, which crawled at the fraudulence of my posture. I was not truly taken in by anyone or anything. I was always able to distinguish what was real from what was not and what was right from what was wrong. I had seen too much dishonesty and unkindness, insecurity and weakness in people, including myself, to respect and revere mere title, celebrity or any accomplishment that produced superficial and entirely selfish benefits.

When I was in my own company, I began to hate myself more and more. I fell into a constant state of panic as I saw the futility of my search for a definition of myself in the world around me. The life I was living was nothing more than a bucket list of events and encounters, not one that would help me construct a new identity and bring quality to my life experience.

Eventually, the artificial confidence injected by Prozac was not enough; my abuse of alcohol took over, especially after I received an education in wine drinking. Along with my parents, I visited all the celebrated chateaux in the famous wine making region of Bordeaux. I met the likes of Baroness Philippine de Rothschild, the owner of Mouton Rothschild, and other proprietors of the grandest vineyards in France: Chateau Lafitte, Petrus, Latour and many more where I drank some of the oldest vintages of the finest wines ever produced. It was a world of its own – glamorous, exciting and one of the most celebrated parts of French national identity that stood right beside their culture of gastronomy – I couldn't have been better positioned to stumble dangerously once again, and fall harder than ever before.

When I began to discover the effects of second degree alcohol abuse, I was captivated by the feeling it generated. All of a sudden I was uninhibited in the concrete reality of my life; under the spell of a subtle high, I felt confident enough to approach people, introduce myself and initiate conversation, no longer hampered by the possibility of rejection.

At the university bar I began to drink heavily, finding release from the life I was play-acting at home, in which I had to be discreet and cautious. With Karl, I graduated from beer to vodka, the effects of which were far more lethal. We would get high at the university bar, and then, with reckless courage, we would go out into the streets of

Paris, into bars and nightclubs where we drank more and more until we fell into an intimacy with each other. Every time I was drunk, I lost the identity I had constructed and the defenses I erected. I would come home feeling both villain and victim of the lies I lived, my pretended pride sucked out of me and shame reinstated.

It was a sinking feeling that vandalized my dignity, my only recourse to fill the vacuumn with as much food as I could. I scavenged for scraps of food in the kitchen, praying it would go undetected the next day by the staff and my mother. When I was safely ensconced in my bathroom, I sat on the cold tiles of the floor where I ate and vomited again and again, until I felt purged of my shame.

On more than one occasion, I fell asleep with my head on the toilet seat, an almost breathless sleep from which I would wake in the early hours of the morning, gasping, my head throbbing violently and my face sullied by dried vomit stuck to my lips. I would clean up the mess as well as I could and wash myself with an almost vicious aggression. I felt no compassion for myself, or pity. I was full of self-loathing each time as I manoeuvred myself into bed and a sleep tortured by the question of how I would face the next day.

At first, the mornings after were without consequences. Karl was unaware of the delayed repercussions of my alcoholism. He could not judge me and he made no demands for intimacy outside the safe confines of a drunken stupor. He did not suffer any guilt, neither from his recreational alcohol abuse nor from minor adultery. Karl was not an addict; he knew who and what he was.

I didn't, and I stayed on that merry-go-round until I fell off it.

As my abuse of alcohol escalated, so did the frequency of bulimia. I was left without control or camouflage and I became an embarrassment to my parents at official receptions and dinner parties. I drank copious amounts of wine that destroyed my resistance to binge eating; I would indelicately ask to be served a second and third time. I would speak out of turn and I slurred each time I did.

When I behaved in such a manner at our residence, I was peremptorily dismissed by my parents. Once again I would hang my head in shame over the toilet seat and vomit with a gruelling force to try and blunt the memory of my behaviour. Finally, my abuse of alcohol became so great, I had no memory at all. I would wake up in the mornings to a blank mind that gradually filled with paranoia.

I developed a stammer in my speech, and I began to get blinding headaches and dizzy spells. Then one day, I extracted the tiny leaflet from inside a box of Prozac; on it, listed as possible side effects were a speech impediment, headaches and dizziness especially when, emphasized the written warning in capital letters, the drug was consumed in tandem with alcohol. Overnight I took myself off the drug, and the withdrawal that ensued, in conjunction with my continued abuse of alcohol, led to a slow and steady descent into the dark depths of despair.

That descent began on a holiday weekend I spent with my parents and brother in Monte Carlo. On our second last night there I drank so much rosé wine that I lost my balance and fell to the ground outside a restaurant at which we were dining. Our hosts had to call an ambulance to take me to the nearest hospital.

When I regained consciousness, I was subjected to a series of tests including a CT scan and an encephalogram, all of which failed to yield any conclusive results. I had, simply, been drunk; I knew the truth but I didn't face it, and neither did my family that day.

A few weeks later, in the early hours of the morning, my father found me in the living room of our residence with several friends, including Karl. I had brought them home with me to continue drinking after a night of vigorous alcohol abuse at bars and nightclubs. We had just graduated from university, an occasion that remains insignificant in my memory. I hadn't informed my parents of the graduation ceremony, such was my shame at the absence of any exceptional academic achievement which might give them pride. When my father exposed me that morning, my shame was grossly magnified.

I was barely lucid as I tried to justify myself to him while he asked the others to leave. Then he told me to go to bed and left me standing in the hallway convulsing with humiliation and self-hatred. I could not go to bed, but I did go to my room carrying a kitchen knife with which I wished to end my life of lies, pretences, addiction and shame. But before I could hurt myself, I fell asleep on the floor of the bathroom.

When I woke up, my father was cradling me gently. He had found me lying on the ground and carried me to my bed. I remained silent as I listened to him blame himself for what had happened, for denying me my fun and embarrassing me in front of my friends. I let him take that blame, as did my mother, and we all chose to deny the truth of my alcoholism and believe the lie of my innocence.

The day that lie could no longer be sustained was the day I was discovered lying on the floor of the guest bathroom. All I remember of the incident is that I had somehow managed to find my way home from a party held the night before; the next morning the staff informed my parents that my bed had not been slept in. They searched all four storeys of the house until they saw my tiny handbag lying on a table in the entrance lobby, which led them to the guest bathroom. The door was locked and my father had to summon the resident handyman to break it open. Behind the door, I lay unconscious on the ground and in a pool of vomit.

TWELVE

'Hi, my name is Diya, and I am an addict.'

I had not been unconscious that day, I was in a drunken sleep from which I wasn't easily stirred. I had little recollection of what had happened the night before, but I remembered being with Karl and doing cartwheels on the sidewalk of the Champs Élysées – a memory aroused by my arms, which ached, even as the rest of me remained painfully hollow.

My mother and father were too frightened to be angry. It was an almost palpable fear that I had generated. I felt a criminal and on bended knees I prayed for deliverance from my shame while my mother silently pleaded for help – her pleas were answered but my prayers went unheard. I did not understand the strength of shame – I had to admit it first but I couldn't. I was trying to fight it, look for an escape from it, and then beg for forgiveness.

I did not receive that forgiveness – instead I was presented with a punishment which came disguised as a solution.

One day, approximately two weeks after that incident, my mother asked me to present myself in the study of the majestic residence that had constituted home for two-and-a-half years. At noon that day, I sat down on one of the armchairs in the study and while I waited for my mother, I looked around the room for what felt like the first time: at the period furniture, the gilded tapestries on the walls, the ornate lamps, the lush carpeting and, through the French windows, the resplendent Eiffel Tower lit by the midday sun, and quietly, I asked myself yet again, 'But what did I do wrong?' I was searching for the answer within myself when, very gently, my mother interrupted me.

A young woman accompanied her, a woman just a few years older than me. She wore a serene expression on a face filled with compassion. I could see that, with her, she brought the promise of a solution – to me it represented a punishment, but one I imagined, would help vindicate my shame. I don't remember her name or nationality. She spoke English fluently and she was someone known to my mother's sister who also lived in Paris. They were part of a group dedicated to life improvement through Buddhist philosophy. The day my aunt discovered the lady was a recovering addict, she called my mother immediately to suggest a meeting. At first I was intrigued, then fascinated, and ultimately frightened by the story I was told that day.

The young woman had been an anorexic-bulimic for most of her life until she hit rock bottom and found herself at the doorstep of a twelve-step programme for recovery. The programme was originally designed to treat alcoholics and later adapted to address all types of addiction.

Before telling us her story, she explained what addiction is and how an eating disorder conforms to the definition. She said that it is thought, but not proved, to be a genetically linked defect of the neuro-transmission systems that rule the reward centres in the brain. It can manifest in the abuse of any kind of substance or compulsive behaviour that alters a person's state of mind and then damages the quality of that person's life. She continued to explain how the defect might be triggered at any stage of life and by any circumstance, and that it cannot either be reversed or cured.

Until her very last words, I had been sitting on the edge of my seat, devouring information that absolved me, not only of the blame I had laid on myself for my condition, but also my continuous nourishment of it, for which I had damned myself for seven years. But the words 'it cannot either be reversed or cured' brought with them a deafening sound, a pronunciation of what felt like a second death sentence in my life. That sound silenced everything around me and all I could hear were the voices in my head arguing with each other, one embracing defeat, the other refusing to by the sheer force of will.

When I was able to hear again, my mother was asking the young woman whether she would like something to eat. She looked at her watch and answered yes, it was time for her third small meal of the day. She asked for two boiled eggs and 50 grams of boiled rice. I was astonished, especially when she went on to explain how her diet would have to be regimented for the rest of her life. All types of white sugar and white flour were prohibited as a result of their trigger effect: a trigger to consume compulsively, which might occasion an episode of equally debilitating denial.

Suddenly my mind was racing; it was questioning the information with both anger and desperation, but I was unable then to find the answer that would help me defy the laws governing recovery from addiction.

I watched intently as the young woman ate her measured quantity of food, at once controlled and compulsive. And I felt deep disgust at her diagnosis and self-proclaimed recovery which she proudly, and almost cruelly, announced was a lifelong journey for each and every addict. But that wasn't where her story ended. It ended at an in-patient treatment centre for addiction called PROMIS, located in Kent, England and that afternoon I found myself nodding my acquiescence to being admitted there.

I returned to my bedroom, a noble wood-panelled room, which had been both shelter and prison in some of the darkest hours of my life. And that day, in my bedroom, I found a new answer to the question that had tormented me for much of my life: 'But what did I do wrong?' The answer was nothing. I had done nothing wrong. Circumstance had triggered a course of evolution I had allowed to define me, a definition I now despised and wanted to break at any cost. The young woman had told me how I could and could not break that definition. But thanks to her, in the privacy of my bedroom, I gave myself what proved to be the greatest gift of all – I forgave myself.

I shut my eyes and, in the shadows of blindness, I was able to detect the silhouettes of the two people who lived within me: me and I. 'Please forgive me, Diya,' I said. And she did. She forgave me and she silently gave permission to my questioning why I could not break those definitions, while I made an equally mute commitment to finding how I could.

Before she left that afternoon, the young woman had advised me to attend anonymous meetings of addict groups held at the American Church of Paris, as a soft introduction to the twelve-step programme for recovery. Later that day, after my mother had spoken with a counselor at PROMIS Recovery Centre in England, to arrange a preliminary visit and assessment, I telephoned the Church to ask when the next addict group meeting was being held.

At eleven o'clock the next morning, I found myself in a windowless room in an annexe of the American Church of Paris; it is located on the Quai d'Orsay, along the left bank of the River Seine, in the immediate vicinity of the French Ministry of Foreign Affairs. But all the majesty of the surrounding area could not lift the pall of misery clouding the four walls of the room in which I grudgingly claimed a seat in a community of people brought together by the deceptive, life-threatening affliction called addiction.

While I waited for the meeting to be convened, I observed the people around me. Some were friendly, the rest, like me, wary and resentful of their place in that world. But the overriding current that all but electrocuted me was of a kind of jingoism in the shared misery that united the people sitting in that room – they appeared to distinguish themselves by it and celebrate a sense of belonging they had been unable to find elsewhere.

I was the only newcomer that day, but I was not received

gently, nor was I welcomed with the kind of reassurance and compassion I expected from fellow addicts already familiar with the trials and tribulations of recovery. Instead, my inaudible reception was that of a new fish by inmates of a prison who revel in the transparent fear and discomfort of the novice. They had all been through it themselves, the result: 'Do unto others as has been done to you.'

The session was abruptly opened by a man named Robert; he took his seat in the circular arrangement of chairs and, boldly and almost proudly, said 'Hi, my name is Robert and I am an addict,' to which the others chanted in unison, 'Hi, Robert.'

It was sinister, the hypnotic atmosphere that gradually permeated the room as the meeting progressed. At first there was a silence that appeared familiar and comforting to everyone present. It was broken by Robert who, noticing my presence, asked me to introduce myself the same way he had done earlier.

I was momentarily paralysed by the idea of defining my entire being by a single word, *addict,* but I did. And with a voice I didn't recognize, I heard myself say, 'Hi, my name is Diya and I am an addict,' to which the automated and perfectly synchronized response was, 'Welcome, Diya.'

For the first time in my life, I didn't want to feel welcome and I didn't want to belong, but I stayed for most of that session which was punctuated by disquieting silences. Some of the people present raised their voices, one at a time, and delivered the same introduction followed by a disclosure of how they were feeling that day. There was no self-examination or discussion in the after-math of each revelation.

I felt both baffled and belligerent in such a farcical environment that promoted the promise of recovery in the absence of any dialogue or debate. I quietly slipped out before the end of the session, my mind swimming with questions, and my heart sinking in despair at another broken promise.

I went to a cafe and ordered as much food as I could. I ate slowly while I stared straight ahead, the weight of despair gradually lifting, then mercifully liquidating as I purged myself of that food inside a rudimentary toilet hidden in a corner of the cafe.

I never went back to the American Church of Paris, but I did move forward, a fortnight later, to PROMIS Recovery Centre in England. I needed to know more, to find out more; my curiosity was a fuel, discharged by my forgiveness of myself and it became my greatest friend on the road less travelled to recovery.

THIRTEEN

'God, grant me the serenity to accept the things I cannot change,
The courage to change the things I can,
And wisdom to know the difference.'

My father drove us there himself, to the beautiful countryside of Kent in England. It was a long drive from Paris to Calais, a ferry ride across the English Channel to Dover, and finally the most arduous stretch as we advanced towards PROMIS Recovery Centre – almost macabre an approach, framed as it was by the lush English countryside that whispered stories of garden parties and picnics in the summertime, not of imprisonment and the search for redemption.

I was without fear, guilt or shame when we entered the grounds of our destination, so sparse in contrast to its environs, almost deliberately trimmed of any visual appeal that might detract from the raison d'être of the recovery centre.

PROMIS has since evolved, but what I remember are two detached buildings, somewhat Tudor in their architectural style, one of them with a small annex which housed an office and a clinic. As we disembarked from the car, a middle-aged man with an uneven gait walked towards us. His name was Paul, he was the office administrator and he and the nurses were the only members of personnel who were not recovering addicts themselves. The method, in what appeared to me was the madness of the treatment programme, was to employ recovering addicts to treat fellow addicts – a method that resembled the use of hunting dogs to pluck a victim from its hiding place. There was an aggression in the approach, even in theory, as explained to us by Paul.

We sat with him in the tiny office, where I was exempt from interrogation as I was seeking admission of my own free will. Instead, we were given a summary of the programme and we learned that the addictive personality generally belongs to people with a high intelligence quotient, those that are natural born leaders and who misuse both traits. I felt unable to digest the statistics in relation to the facts of my life, until they were further illustrated by Paul, and I watched my parents find solace in the detailing, which, all too robustly, resonated with them.

Once again, both guilt and shame were detonated, obliterating the courage and dignity with which I had arrived. I had been obliged to listen to a discourse on the lies and manipulations, the convincing pretences and denials of the addictive personality, its cruelty and criminality no less than second-degree murder of the self and of those who befriend, love and care for that self. And suddenly I understood the madness, the many hiding places of the hunted, for whom the only able hunter is a recovering addict able to detect and destroy those hiding places otherwise invisible to the naked and uninitiated eye.

But this was not only the story of an addict. It was an illustration of human beings sullied by the instinct for lies, deceptions, betrayals and cruelty as they – we – flounder for that evasive feeling of control, for dictatorship over the shape and destiny of our beings and our lives. A seed was then planted, but my appreciation of a context much larger than myself, much greater than my own life, did not flower till many years later.

I looked at my parents that day. I really looked at them and felt an unprecedented surge of love and gratitude, followed by the birth of a fierce instinct, an instinct to protect them first and foremost from myself. It injected new energy into my journey forward on which I often tripped but did not again fall.

Paul terminated his lecture with subtle sensitivity. Our appetites for information had been satiated, and anything more might have been indigestible. We followed him out of the office and into the central building on the property. There were several bedrooms for the patients, two lounges, a group meeting room, a kitchen and a dining hall – an innocent image lending a warm welcome, betrayed only by the presence of a lone coin-operated telephone booth.

Paul pre-empted my query – revealed by the expression of terror on my countenance – his explanation one I wished I had never provoked. He gently told me that patients were not allowed any contact with the outside world except by one telephone call from that one telephone booth on one day of the week. However, on Sundays, family members and chosen friends were permitted to visit, have lunch and stay until the late afternoon.

The patients were not allowed to carry any personal devices, mobile telephones, Walkmans or any other instrument for playing music or watching movies. They were not given access to any reading material other than literature on addiction and recovery and there was no extra-curricular activity permitted at the individual level except for the study and contemplation of treatment and recovery. Even the small gymnasium on the premises had been sealed as a result of abuse of the facility: the exercise-induced adrenalin high constituted a mind-altering activity that distracted from the treatment.

The programme was designed to submerge and suffocate the addicts in reflection upon their addictions while they were kept in confinement and until their withdrawal was complete. I already knew all too well that the expulsion of addiction was considered non-viable.

It was a veritable miniature police state in which choice was confiscated. But even in the quagmire of my terror, I could not help wondering if the ability to make the right choice was exhibited, and how it could be cemented in its absence.

We continued on our tour and I was introduced to other citizens of that state who appeared to possess a quiet nationalist sentiment that was encouraging. It was different to the atmosphere at the American Church in Paris, which was polluted by the showmanship of misery. That showmanship was forced by the confessional nature of those meetings in which consolation was fleeting and the moment you left, abstinence became a difficult, if not impossible, promise to keep. At the recovery centre, there was a real sense of community and lasting consolation that lingered beyond treatment. Loneliness was spared, reality was in the now, and by that definition, common to all.

Yet, what was more frightening at PROMIS than at the American Church in Paris was that real life did not creep in at all. At the Church, people had been almost indifferent to the plight of others as they grasped at straws of time away from the daily grind of their lives poisoned by addiction. At PROMIS, far more discomfiting was the overstated welcome and demonstration of love by people who appeared to suffer from temporary amnesia of their individual realities.

The similarity to the synthetic world conjured up by drug abuse was such that I stiffened and felt my stomach turn when I was embraced by a lady called Kate, a cocaine addict. It was a tight embrace tainted by the eerie reception into a cult that presupposes the sacrifice of individuality. I had felt it before, and that feeling momentarily shook my commitment to my own recovery.

PROMIS was a virtual laboratory structured to brainwash and redesign the minds of addicts before releasing them into the world with a motor driven by an unwavering belief in the twelve steps, which remained unknown to me. When the sickening sentiment of self-sacrifice passed, my curiosity was generously restored and I contemplated the efficacy of a programme that claimed success in the treatment of all addiction and compulsive behaviour with a singular protocol.

I was introduced to a cocaine addict, an overeater, an anorexic – so weak she could not hold her head upright as she greeted me – a relationship addict, heroin addicts, alcoholics and many others with single or multiple addictions and compulsive behaviours. Not once, in Paul's introduction, was there any mention of customized treatment for an individual.

I felt increasingly threatened by the environment, but slowly I managed to rehabilitate my own courage and banish any resistance to the possibility of recovery. Suddenly a gong sounded, heralding lunchtime and Paul ushered us into the dining hall. With the exception of those suffering from eating disorders, all the patients and counselors were expected to serve themselves. We took our places and my parents were invited to the buffet while I remained seated.

A few moments later I was presented with a pre-plated serving of food, identical to that given to each patient suffering from an eating disorder. I was told that allowances were made only for food allergies and intolerance; all other inclinations and aversions were unilaterally disregarded. I felt choked as I swallowed my first bite of grilled salmon and sautéed broccoli, but I was determined to retain what I ate, to surrender myself to the programme and give it every chance. My mind went into battle with my digestive system, unused to assimilating any food other than boiled peas and carrots, and my eyes welled with tears.

They were tears of lost hope for a cushioned introduction to my treatment. But I did not allow those tears to spill. I saw the expressions of sorrow and guilt on the faces of my parents as they watched me grapple under public scrutiny, and I became firm in my resolve to persevere with the programme and save them from bearing witness to my struggle.

Paul sat next to me at lunch and I told him I would return alone, unaccompanied by my parents. Then I asked him if someone could collect me from the train station. He declared me a brave girl and said that he would come to fetch me himself. I had finished nearly all the food on my plate, the retention inescapable not only under so many watchful eyes but also on the drive back to Paris, a drive I could only hope to take again as a recovered addict.

Before we left, it was agreed that I would return ten days later, after a hefty payment had been made to the centre for an initial treatment period of six weeks. I felt nauseated by the cost of my treatment, but for my parents, it was far smaller a price to pay than that of my addiction, which risked all our lives.

It was a long journey home for what were the shortest ten days of my life, ten days that held both threat and opportunity, the duality exhausting. I felt almost numb as I anticipated my voluntary incarceration.

My mother didn't want me to go alone but I was immoveable in my decision. I could not, and would not, put her through the kind of regressive responsibility from which she, like any other parent with a child of my age, should have been freed. I felt it my duty to relieve my parents of the hold I had on them, even as I continued to hold them close.

On the eleventh day, I packed my little bag and in the official car of the Indian ambassador to France, flanked by my mother and father, I went to the Gare du Nord railway station in Paris. I was to take the Eurostar to Ashford where Paul would be waiting for me.

The atmosphere at the Gare du Nord sparkled with long-awaited arrivals and the excitement of departures and I felt both mocked and aggressed by the environment as I waited to board my train. Very abruptly, I remember, boarding was announced, shaking my parents and myself out of our reverie and into the cold reality and reason for our separation. But I do not remember our goodbyes, and neither do they.

My next memory is of sitting in a near-empty cabin of the Eurostar, where I finally gave release to my tears. I cried and cried until I felt emptied of my past and cleansed for my future, a future I had never considered before that day, drowned as I had been by the tidal wave of my here and now.

Paul was waiting at the other end, his posture reserved, as if to protect him from any emotional involvement with a patient. He greeted me without welcome or warning and as much as his demeanour was benign in its outline, I felt paralysed by the implication as I was about to get into the car. He held the door open for me, but I refused to get in until he made me a promise. And he did.

Forty-five minutes later I hurriedly unpacked my bag in one of the bedrooms on the first floor of PROMIS and then rushed down to the late afternoon group meeting. The session was opened by Alan, the head counsellor, and everyone stood up from their chairs, arranged in the same kind of circle I had seen at the American Church. But at the recovery centre we were expected to hold hands and say a prayer. I was given a piece of paper with the words written on it – they were the words of the serenity prayer, a virtual anthem of the twelve-step programme for recovery.

When I finished reciting those words, for the first time in twenty-three years of my life, I felt the power of relief and the relief of surrender.

> *God, grant me the serenity to accept the things I cannot change, The courage to change the things I can, And wisdom to know the difference.*

FOURTEEN

Step 1 – *We admitted we were powerless over our addiction –*
that our lives had become unmanageable.

Step 2 – *We came to believe that a Power greater than*
ourselves could restore us to sanity.

Step 3 – *We made a decision to turn our will and our lives*
over to the care of God as we understood God.

I have a frighteningly vivid memory of my first night.
I woke up in a panic, dripping with sweat. It was dark
grey, not black, when I pressed the light button on my
alarm clock to see if dawn was imminent. I had brought
my alarm clock with me from home. I had become
dependent on time; it helped me determine when I could
secretly binge, and when I had to erase proof of my food
and substance abuse.

But in my new habitat, the purpose of the clock was
altogether different. It was meant to help me rise before
the others – to facilitate private access to one of the
few common bathrooms on the premises. Each time I
retained any nourishment, the flawed functioning of my
body was disturbed and I struggled to expel waste from
my system.

After my first visit to PROMIS, where I had eaten the biggest meal I retained in many years, I suffered through the night from a stomach that cramped in a way which can only be described as corrupt and a mind dripping the kind of torture it does in the face of change and the breaking of a habit. That same night, the voice of the addict had been merciless in the stories she spun of what would happen to me if I didn't purge myself of the nourishment.

A battle ensued between my rational mind and gut instinct. It wasn't just my battle but one fought often and by many who may not be cursed with a specific affliction. It is a battle that must become a dialogue, which helps furnish the best result for both mind and instinct; it is not meant to instigate the relinquishing of control by one to the other. But mine was a damaged gut in which instinct had been perverted by a frightened child, and that night I chose to listen to the flawless reasoning of a rational mind, which asked me to have patience.

It took two days for me to be able to go to the bathroom, two days in which I was crucified by an abdomen that convulsed continuously and by blinding headaches as my mind fought my body to comply with the laws of biology. Eventually it did, but with both resistance and pain, and I was forced to acknowledge the impossible durability of willpower against the onslaught of defiled instinct.

That first night at PROMIS, I was roused from my sleep by a dramatic dance of words in my head, those from steps one to three of the twelve-step programme for recovery. It turned out to be just past midnight, the colour of night compromised by a floodlit central courtyard just below my bedroom window – a reminder of the prison to which I had surrendered myself. I was unable to go back to sleep and in my mind, I replayed the proceedings of the previous evening while the voice of my other screamed inside my gut, telling me to run away as fast as I could.

After the group therapy session, the patients had been freed from treatment for the rest of that day, required to reunite at dinner time. I didn't know what to do with myself, but I welcomed the temporary freedom from my peers with whom an inescapable connection had been foisted on me.

As it happened, my freedom was short-lived; the patients began to approach me to introduce themselves and extend welcome. Each did in a manner so different, I found myself riding a turbulent wave that rose with promise and sank with disappointment. Some welcomed me as if it was my homecoming and others showed contempt. The latter were there against their will, the denial of addiction firmly indoctrinated and their disdain for the treatment programme incontrovertible. Then there were some like Patrick, a young cocaine addict in whose greeting I sensed a strong will to recover but a fragile commitment to the treatment, in spite of his blind belief in the cogency of the twelve-step programme.

I did not feel a natural affinity to any group but for the first time, and thereafter for the rest of my life, I stopped trying to belong. By default, the tug of war between my rational mind and instinct had engendered a personal commitment to recovery; I no longer wished for either support or companionship on my journey.

I managed, discreetly, to withdraw to the lounge that was scattered with books on addiction, recovery, life philosophy and meditations for recovering addicts. The others went about their appointed duties in service of the treatment centre, did personal chores such as laundry or wandered out into the garden for a gentle stroll.

I was not alone in the lounge. Patrick was there, sitting upright on a sofa, his eyes shut and his expression tortured. He briefly opened his eyes to acknowledge me. They were a vibrant aquamarine colour, set in a devastatingly handsome face from which I immediately recoiled – I had been warned against intimate relationships with my fellow patients. It was considered as much of a misdemeanour as an attempt at physical exercise, or a detached approach to treatment called 'going through the motions'.

Paul had delivered those warnings on our drive from the train station, his voice feeble, embarrassed by such an announcement. I didn't know whether to laugh with bitter sarcasm or scream frantically at the almost Fabian tactics designed to deprive, isolate and crumble a patient beyond the call of duty of the treatment centre; but I listened carefully and reserved both judgement and response.

In the lounge, I gathered a pile of books and a manuscript on which the twelve steps were listed underneath a summary of their origin and evolution. I began to read, but I stopped at step three as the echo of a question reverberated in my mind, a question that comprised one word: How? I shut my eyes as the echo subsided, leaving a stabbing headache in its wake. Then I began to rub my forehead and press my scalp, when I heard Patrick say, 'You know, it works if you work it; that's why I keep coming back.' I looked up at him as I silently repeated his words to myself, and all of a sudden I began to unravel the twelve-step programme for recovery on what was my very first day at PROMIS.

'But then why do you need to keep coming back?' I asked. His answer was ominously withheld. The gong had sounded, announcing dinner time and giving Patrick an excuse for a hasty departure.

I followed him into the dining room and took my place at the table reserved for patients with eating disorders. I was alone for a few minutes but I didn't feel awkward; I felt strong and self-reliant. I knew how much I wanted to recover and I was determined to translate and mould the twelve steps for recovery into my life story, but I refused to let them become my life story. I would not let addiction define me forever.

The spell of strength infused by my thoughts was broken by the arrival of the other patients. I did not want to reveal myself yet, not until I was sure. There was idle chatter at first, to which I listened intently. I didn't participate until I heard one of the patients call out a name – Henrietta. She was absent from the table but I remembered her from my first visit to PROMIS: a frail, vastly undernourished girl who suffered from anorexia and limped without any apparent injury. I learned that she was also a heroin addict, and when I asked where she was, a lady named Jenna answered in a voice unnaturally devoid of empathy: 'She is probably slouching in the courtyard.' I was immediately silenced.

The next time I was addressed, it was by a young man named Henry; he asked me what kind of eating disorder I suffered from. We had just been presented with our pre-plated serving of food consisting of wild rice, grilled chicken and roasted vegetables. I wished then that I had declared myself vegetarian; it would have been easier for my digestive system to contend with. But I knew very little about nutrition, an education in which, I discovered later, is invaluable for recovery from an eating disorder.

I forgot to answer Henry. I was consumed by my thoughts as I stared at the plate of food before me. A few seconds later, I heard him say that it was all right and what I needed to do was to eat slowly.

'I suffer from anorexia-bulimia,' I answered his earlier question, suddenly antagonized by the unsolicited advice. He smiled knowingly at my aggression, interpreting it as anger about my present situation – he assumed it had been imposed on me. Needless to say he was wrong but I let him believe he was right.

What I was really angry about was how easy it all was in a simulated environment where choice did not pose a threat and patients were all but bludgeoned into believing that this form of treatment had no equal or alternative. I was angry at Jenna's brutal dismissal of Henrietta's absence. And I was angry that no one at the table had defended Henrietta, by way of explanation for her whereabouts. But I swallowed all the anger as I began to eat, assuaged by food as was my habit, and by a plan formulating in my mind.

I needed to locate Henrietta and talk to her, to find out

why she was exempt from meal times and to ask her why she wasn't trying. I felt I needed to uncover what hurt her so much.

In the meantime, I returned to the present for fear of betraying my thoughts and politely, I reciprocated Henry's curiosity. In a steady voice and with a softened tone I asked him about his poison.

It turned out that Henry was seated at our table out of choice. He said, all too innocently, that he had returned to PROMIS for the fourth time, this time to treat his addiction to relationships. Earlier he had been admitted for an addiction to overeating, something his lean and athletic frame did not divulge, and for prescription drug abuse. He hesitantly added that his primary addiction was to being a submissive in relationships and he had cross-addictions to food and drugs.

The notion of cross-addiction was not entirely alien to me. But what did alienate and terrify me was the virtual vigil, advanced by such a theory, that each person labelled an addict would have to keep in the pursuit of all self-prescribed needs and pleasures. That label, on which I had found a diagnosis of my problem and reassurance of a solution, suddenly began to feel like a tattoo of identification similar to those that had been worn by prisoners of war in Nazi concentration camps – the kind of identification that would shackle me for the rest of my life.

I must have looked devastated for Henry to offer words of comfort: he told me I would understand everything better when I completed the questionnaire on addiction the following morning. It had been developed by the founder of PROMIS, Dr Robert Lefevre, himself a recovering addict.

I had finished all the food on my plate as I was accustomed to doing, but without my customary conclusion to a meal, I was filled with dread at the thought of the punishment that would be inflicted on my body by such deceit. It was the only meal I had to retain that day but the next day, and every day after that, I would have to face, ingest and digest three meals. The very thought made me silently say the words of the serenity prayer as I excused myself from the table and left the dining room. Behind me, I heard Jenna bellow, 'Don't even think about going to the bathroom' – words of prey, rather than encouragement, which urged me forward in my quest to find Henrietta.

She wasn't in the courtyard and I was about to abandon my search when I saw her coming out of the clinic. She was looking down at her right arm as she unrolled one of the sleeves of her lumberjack shirt. She had been wearing the same shirt the first time we met. It hung heavy on her emaciated frame which could not be obscured by any type or size of garment. She limped to a sunny spot where, with the help of the wall, she lowered herself to the ground. My heart bled as I watched her and I didn't realize I was staring until she looked up, squinting against the sun, and smiled a winsome smile that invited me to join her. I was timid in my approach, afraid to enter her world and guilty of invading her privacy, but she patted the ground beside her encouragingly.

For a while we sat side by side, both still and silent. Then I looked down at the ground as she lifted her face to the sky, shut her eyes and rested her head against the wall. 'It's just a matter of a few days now, and they will let me go,' she said, and went on to explain that all her vital signs had been checked at the clinic and they were rapidly diminishing.

'But why?' I asked. 'Don't you want to get better?'

She opened her eyes and turned to look at me, those light brown pupils far away, buried in pain, and she said, 'No. I want my high. I need my high. I can't live without my high, not like this. I don't understand it here, but you will. You are different, different from the others … I can tell. You will figure it out and you will be okay.' I tried to argue but she held up her hand, the bones of her fingers visible beneath the transparent skin, and she said, 'When you find the answers, and the way, come and look for me.'

With those words I knew I was dismissed. I lifted myself up from the ground to stand before Henrietta, both desperate and determined to help her, but words failed me as I tried to make a promise I was afraid I wouldn't keep. I turned around and began to walk away, then I stopped and tried to summon the courage to return to her, but I couldn't.

A few hours later, Henrietta was found lying in the corridor outside her bedroom. She had fainted. She was alive and breathing when an ambulance came to take her away. I stood at my bedroom window and watched her go, and with tears streaming down my face, I said a silent goodbye, punctuated by the promise that I would find a way.

FIFTEEN

'The best way out is always through.'
— Robert Frost

My thoughts returned to the present and I was overwhelmed by helplessness. I had made a promise I intended to keep, but I didn't know how. What I did know was in the mind and makeup of an addict, where there is only will, there is no way.

Step three told us to turn our will over to God – *but how*, I asked myself repeatedly, my head beginning to throb again. Step two said that the belief in a power greater than ourselves would restore us to sanity, but it didn't tell us how. How were we to arrive at that belief?

I told myself God could not be the premise; He had to be the outcome, when rationale retreated and explanation expired. I knew I could not turn my will over to God without finding Him first, without understanding Him. It was to the treatment centre that I would surrender my will, all too finite in the absence of any translation. Henrietta had recognized the shortcomings of the programme and given up. Patrick, like many of the others, just kept coming back. I needed to investigate the matter further but as dawn broke, I first had to contend with my own body.

I lifted my T-shirt and looked down at my swollen abdomen. I stroked it gently and it felt taut, stubborn and defensive. I was weary but alert when I made my way to the bathroom at the end of the corridor outside my bedroom. I was lucky to have a room to myself, albeit temporarily; a patient had been discharged just before my arrival. It was quiet at five in the morning. We were not expected to present ourselves downstairs until seven, by which time all the patients were expected to be bathed and dressed for the day. We were not permitted to return to the rooms until bedtime, unless for special reasons and under supervision.

An hour later, my body hadn't relented but at the sound of voices outside the bathroom, I gave up. Very quickly I showered, dressed and made my way downstairs. I was clad in checked cotton pants and a T-shirt. I had brought four sets with me from home to wear as one does a uniform. They were a size big for me, allowing for an increase in weight, an eventuality I so feared but which my uniform would help enshroud while I pursued recovery.

My head was pounding while I waited downstairs for the dreaded gong to sound. The patients on breakfast duty were there already, and I watched them as they performed their tasks robotically. Their faces were inanimate and, just by looking at them, I felt both disdain and desperation. I knew I did not belong in that plastic environment, and I had to will myself forward into the dining room when breakfast was boldly broadcasted.

To my surprise, I was given a choice between a continental and an English breakfast, the latter an intimidating composition of eggs, hash browns, grilled tomatoes and toast. I chose the former with alacrity, a more accessible compilation of cereal, wholewheat toast and a piece of fruit. But even within the continental offering, I had to make a choice and I was stymied. For such a long time it had not mattered what I liked – I had always eaten indiscriminately and I didn't even know what I truly liked, my choices having been unimpeded by any barometer including taste. Suddenly I felt jeopardized by the effect my choice of food might have on my weight and digestive system. Fortunately Jenna came to my rescue.

Jenna, Henry and all the other patients labelled with an eating disorder belonged to a subset called, 'overeaters'. In their forceful, yet rarely fruitful, crusade against weight gain, they had learned a little about diet and nutrition. Jenna guided me towards Weetabix cereal with soya milk, whole wheat toast with Marmite and a banana, none of which I had ever eaten before. And for the first time in several years, I tasted what I ate.

The crisp wheat-grain cereal slowly dissolved in the soya milk, and as I ate I was intrigued by the textures and flavours that unfolded on my palate. At first the cereal biscuits were almost thorny and salty, but they softened and sweetened when they absorbed the milk. The wholewheat toast with Marmite was meaty in flavour, perfectly positioned as a second course to my breakfast, and finally the banana, a welcome conclusion that cleansed my palate and mellowed the passage of food down my intestinal tract. I was momentarily transported by the symphony of sensations until my gut twisted sharply, rebelling against the nourishment.

Immediately I shut my eyes. They were brimming with tears as my will waged war against the instinct to expel the food I had consumed. Once again, my will conquered. I had entrusted it to the treatment center, which sequestered the possibility of expulsion. But on my second day at PROMIS, I knew with absolute certainty that the sheer power of will could not be sustained.

For seven years of my life, my instinct had denied me choice and championed my pursuit of a path of self-destruction. Now the treatment centre expropriated that same choice and coerced its patients into surrendering their will as the answer to recovery from addiction. All too proudly PROMIS advertised the concept 'HALT' – never allow yourself to get Hungry, Angry, Lonely and Tired – but it refused to address the birth and management of those feelings.

Neither the victory nor the surrender of will is adequate in the face of villainous instinct. That is true, not only for an addict, but also many others living in a world where choice has become an epidemic in the absence of guidance by a healthy instinct – that instinct has, at best, been blunted by the intellect and paralysed by convention and, at worst, damaged by circumstance.

The treatment centre could neither bury nor amputate the instinct to self-destruct. It was the very nucleus of the sickness, and had to be healed. But the propagators of the twelve-step programme declared it untreatable. I refused to believe that. Unknown to me then, there was a part of my instinct that had been left untarnished and it is what helped save me from a wounded life.

As the spasms in my gut began to settle, all those thoughts germinated in my mind, forming a puzzle I had yet to solve. Often I had heard people say they had been driven by an instinct for something, which yielded success. Somewhere in the labyrinth of ideas populating my mind, I knew it was an example of a perfect duet played by a healthy instinct and a muscular will – an example I wanted to follow.

I left the dining room wearier than when I had arrived, but I felt exhilarated by the glimmer of an answer I had seen in my mind's eye.

I made my way to the lounge where I was to answer the questionnaire on addiction. While I waited for one of the counselors to present me with the document, I began to read the manuscript listing the twelve steps. This time I stopped at step eleven and I read it again, and again and again …

Step 11 – We sought through prayer and meditation to improve our conscious contact with God as we understood God, praying only for knowledge of God's will for us and the power to carry that out.

… And there it was: my answer. I became convinced that it was to be my first and final step towards recovery and freedom. I just needed to find my way to that step.

Robert, one of the counsellors, came into the lounge

and handed me the questionnaire. He advised me to contemplate each question thoroughly and answer it honestly. I didn't need that advice. I had no resistance to recovery. Unlike Henrietta, I didn't want my high, I didn't need it any more. But I did want a high, the kind I had seen in Muhammad Ali many years earlier, and I did not wish to either amputate or restrain my instinct for it. Mollified by that thought, I opened the questionnaire and began to read.

On each page, there was an examination of a patient's relationship with a particular addiction – the first, with alcohol. It appeared harmless enough, and I answered the questions with a yes or no as I was meant to. 'Do you find that one drink tends to not satisfy you but you want more?' *YES*. 'Do you use alcohol as both a comfort and strength?' *YES*. And so it went on until I had answered all the questions on the first page. I was well aware that the computation would prove my cross-addiction to alcohol.

The second section was on nicotine addiction and for an instant I stopped. I was confused by the inclusion of nicotine in a group of mind-altering substances and behaviours. Before answering, I read all the questions, many of them the same as in the first section: 'Do you tend to use nicotine as both a comfort and a strength?' 'Do you often use nicotine significantly more than you intend?' I turned the page without answering and I kept turning the pages until I reached the end of the questionnaire. It was, in fact, a document provoking the worst kind of self-examination that could be nothing but damaging.

There were sixteen categories in which mind-altering

and life-threatening compulsions were examined. In each category, the questions were leading ones that sought to uncover, if not insist upon, the presence of a compulsive tendency, whether or not benign in its impact on the individual.

The sixteen categories were alcohol, nicotine, recreational drugs, food bingeing, food starving, exercise, caffeine, shopping-spending-stealing, gambling and risk taking, workaholism, prescription drug addiction, sex-love addiction, dominant relationship addiction, submissive relationship addiction, dominant compulsive helping and submissive compulsive helping.

I flipped through the pages again, feeling disoriented by the kind of questions asked, to which an answer by a mere yes or no could so easily be misinterpreted. In the category of exercise, there were questions asking whether I preferred to exercise alone or in company and if I often felt tension and excitement when I was about to exercise. My answer to both was yes but I refused to believe that made me an exercise addict. Under the heading of submissive compulsive helping, there was a question asking if I tried to avoid upsetting other people regardless of the consequences to myself to which my answer was, once again, yes. In the category of workaholism, there was a question asking if I tended to tidy up the mess that someone else had got into at work, even when I had not been asked to. I had never held a real job but I knew my answer would be yes. And No, I began to scream inside my head. No, I am not a workaholic. No, I am not a submissive compulsive helper. No, I am not addicted to exercise ...

Finally, in a fatigue-induced trance I answered all the questions and when I emerged, I felt fearless and driven. The questionnaire thrived on fear, on instilling in a person the fear of being injured and prescribing bandages for wounds that did not exist. I was not going to fall victim to such a practice. I was an addict, addicted to escape from my wounds and from myself. I had come to PROMIS to face my fears and remove my bandages and that was what I was going to do.

Suddenly my purpose was clear – to question the policies of the treatment centre and the theories it tendered. The twelve-step programme had many merits but its instruction was vastly flawed and I intended to redesign it by example. I had to do it for Henrietta, for myself and for others before and after me, unable to work the machinery of the programme.

SIXTEEN

*'Purpose is the reason for your journey. Passion is the fire
that lights your way.'*

– Anonymous

Henrietta died. Paul entered the meeting room at the end
of the last group therapy session of the day to deliver the
news that impaled my spirit.

I looked up at him and I could not find an expression
of sorrow that reflected my own – neither in his face nor
in any of the faces around me. We were asked by Robert
to hold hands and observe a minute's silence in honour
of Henrietta's life. I did as we were asked and, quietly, I
began to cry. I cried from the pit of my gut where I had
felt the glimmer of an answer I hoped to take to Henrietta
one day.

When the minute passed, I rushed out of the meeting
room and into the garden where I continued to cry,
releasing sounds that were guttural, painful to my own
ears. I knelt on the ground and began tearing at
blades of grass, as if to extract the pain from myself, but
I couldn't until all the tears were shed, leaving behind a
drought of emotion. I sat on the grass and stared ahead,

feeling nothing, nothing at all, while my rational mind took on a momentum of its own – analysing, questioning, judging and executing – until Henry came to find me. He was followed, moments later, by the two youngest patients at the recovery centre. They were Kenny and Melinda, sixteen and fifteen years old respectively, both there against their will.

'Diya,' Henry said. 'We are not monsters. You need to understand that it's about letting go, that's why we are all here.' He sat down on the grass beside me while Melinda and Kenny hovered, hoping to find support from me in their rejection of the programme.

They were just kids, rebels without a cause and they appeared to be unscathed by life. It made me wonder about the logic used to admit them into a recovery programme based solely on their experimental use of cocaine and alcohol. But I held my curiosity at bay while I listened to Henry, who was clearly giving me advice considered impermissible by those that governed the treatment centre.

In barely audible whispers, he told me we were not at PROMIS to help one another but to help ourselves, that Henrietta had refused help and her refusal threatened the treatment and recovery of the other patients.

I couldn't accept what Henry was saying. He was telling me to surrender my rational mind and sever emotion for the sake of recovery, but when emotion resurfaced, as it always does, what was I meant to do? I asked him, and I myself answered: 'Do I drink, take drugs, starve, vomit ... what? What do I do when those feelings come back? Survival is based on instinct, Henry, and my instinct knows only one way. It protected me for a long time until it turned on me. I need to retrain my instinct, not subdue it, and you know I am right.'

Henry didn't argue with me. He stood up with an air of defeat, his final words to me, 'Just give it a chance. If there's one thing you will learn here, it is that there is no nobility in guilt and we do not allow shame to fester, nor do we indulge fear. We must never cower before those sentiments, nor find false absolution from them. They nourish our addictions.'

I understood him and the notions he put before me, relevant not only to addicts but to all human beings who are stifled by fear and believe the feeling of shame, or guilt, in itself qualifies as repentance. The power of the twelve-step programme, in fact lies in steps four to ten; they force the addict to tackle and expunge those feelings, the most debilitating and damaging to a person's soul.

Step 4 – made a searching and fearless moral inventory of ourselves.

Step 5 – admitted to God, to ourselves and to another human being the exact nature of our wrongs.

Step 6 – were entirely ready to have God remove all these defects of character.

Step 7 – humbly asked God to remove our shortcomings.

Step 8 – made a list of all persons we had harmed, and became willing to make amends to them all.

Step 9 – made direct amends to such people wherever possible, except when to do so would injure them or others.

Step 10 – continued to take personal inventory and when we were wrong promptly admitted it.

The hard part was getting to step four.

As Henry walked away, Melinda bounded up to me and announced that they were all a bunch of nutters. Kenny tried to restrain her but I reassured him by laughing at her indiscretion and, partially, I agreed with her. It was easy to believe they were all just a bunch of nutters.

Melinda was a short, chubby and cherubic fifteen-year-old with a mop of blonde hair, twinkling blue eyes, a fiery spirit and a sharp tongue. She made me laugh, and she continued to mend my spirit with her constant natter about how she missed her pot noodles at 'this zoo' with 'this bunch of monkeys'.

We broke into a stroll on the manicured lawns of the recovery centre, and Kenny asked me why I had been forced to come to PROMIS. I answered that no one had forced me to come; I knew I was sick and I didn't want to be sick any more. Then I spoke about my parents as my greatest protectors and friends. Both he and Melinda looked at me, perplexed, and asked me why I was questioning the programme if I knew I was sick and wanted to get better. I explained that I did not wish to replace one addiction with another. I did not want to be dependent on, nor imprisoned by, the twelve-step programme. They couldn't understand what I was saying and I stopped. I didn't wish to either influence or confuse them, especially when Melinda loudly trumpeted her opinion that PROMIS had killed Henrietta.

I stopped walking and turned to look straight into her blue eyes, which had become overcast by asphyxiated grief and muffled fear. Kenny told her to shut up, but she went on to say that PROMIS wanted to send Henrietta away because the centre would have been compromised had she died on the premises, and that was all they cared about, their own survival.

There was a harsh truth in what Melinda said. It represented the universal truth of each man for himself, like it was at PROMIS, dressed and disguised in the cloth of community. I sympathized with Melinda but I knew it was not an absolute truth – PROMIS had not killed Henrietta but they had made her believe there was no other way.

I put my hand on Melinda's shoulder and gently asked what had brought her to PROMIS. The answer jolted me. She told me the courts sent her to PROMIS because she had killed a girl while she was under the influence of alcohol. She looked at me with a stubborn expression, but in her eyes I saw a plea for forgiveness as she proceeded to tell me that it was a mistake. The girl had been making advances towards her boyfriend in a bar, and Melinda had hit her on the head with a beer bottle but she hadn't intended to kill her.

I looked Melinda in the eye, seeing right through her, into the core of a child who would be ruined by her exile at PROMIS, by the label she had been given and the dogmas to which she was prematurely being exposed. She needed something else, as did Kenny, who confessed that he did not know if he was an addict. He said he had no choice but to believe that he was. His parents had forced him into the recovery centre when they discovered he was stealing money from them to go to nightclubs where he would drink a lot of alcohol and take cocaine. 'I think they just don't want me around,' he said, and Melinda nodded in agreement.

My heart broke listening to the two of them. I wanted to hold them close and tell them it was okay, but I didn't possess the faculties to do so. This wasn't about addiction. This was about life, and I myself had neither age nor experience on my side. What I did have was a reason to recover and a place to go back to when I did – I had a loving family and a secure home, both things uncertain for the two young people standing in front of me.

Kenny asked me if my parents were coming to see me on Sunday, and I said no. I had not spoken to them and asked them to visit. It was Friday, the day we were allowed to make our weekly telephone call, but I had avoided doing so. I wanted to protect my parents from an account of the roller coaster I had been riding since my arrival just a day and a half earlier. But when Kenny told me that PROMIS helped the families and friends of patients more effectively than the patients themselves, I realized that my defence of my parents was entirely misplaced.

It was nearly dinner time and I ran to the telephone booth to call my mother and ask her and my father to visit me on Sunday. As I spoke to her, I was overcome by a surge of emotion I was unable to decode. Dinner had been announced and there was urgency in our conversation, brevity that fostered an exchange brimming with sentiment – something I was being starved of at the centre.

When I hung up the telephone, I felt my sanity restored. My parents represented the life I had been given and PROMIS was a flagship for my other life, the one

I had chosen, the one I no longer wanted. The method of treatment to which I had been exposed appeared to unilaterally declare maleficent every aspect of my existence before my surrender to PROMIS. I knew that wasn't true and I had to create an intersection of my two lives if I wanted to change direction and walk my own way to recovery, unaided by any crutch and unconstrained by the canons of the treatment center.

It was my fourth day at PROMIS, and as I lay in bed waiting for dawn to break, I translated the emotions by which I had been engulfed the evening before: courage and conviction.

I had consumed my third meal of the day fearless of punishment and convinced of triumph. I had refused the offer of a natural laxative to ease my discomfort, I had thrown away my cigarettes in an effort to examine the theory of nicotine addiction, and that morning I was going to eliminate caffeine from my diet to test the notion of caffeine dependence.

I vowed to surrender myself to the methods used by the centre, to study them, understand them and overrule them. PROMIS forced a road map to recovery on which it warned of the constant presence of an enemy; we were being taught to avoid that enemy through the ritualistic practice of the twelve steps. But it was not the road map I wanted. I wanted the one that had been given to me, the one without an enemy, the one I shared with my family and on which I hoped to forge other lasting relationships.

The secret to my surrender was to starve my enemy of all that nourished it, to expose it and make it my friend. Even greater than courage and conviction, what I had found was hope, the beauty of which is that it requires no explanation and does not necessitate exhibition. Some years earlier I had been introduced to the idea of hope, a simple but persuasive sentiment.

It was in New York City and I had been invited to the home of a gentleman by the name of Nicholas Vreeland, a young American photographer turned Tibetan Buddhist monk. I had met him briefly in Paris and he had at once detected the troubled waters on which I was trying to sail, but we didn't discuss it. He simply asked me to get in touch with him if I ever visited New York.

I telephoned Nicholas the very morning I arrived in Manhattan, having spent the entire duration of the flight from Paris drinking copious amounts of wine to drown my despair and cheat my loneliness. I did not need to make any polite conversation or explain myself. The anguish in my voice was enough for him to ask me to come straight to his apartment located on the Upper East Side.

I didn't hesitate. Without taking a shower or brushing my teeth, I raced out of the apartment I was staying at in Gramercy Park and made my way uptown.

Nicholas welcomed me into his majestic home with open arms. He gently took my hand and led me into a vast living room where an elderly gentleman was sitting at a writing table set against one of the three French windows that framed the room. He was Tibetan, and Nicholas introduced him as his Rinpoche, his teacher. I held out my hand and he took it in a tight grip that appeared to explore me. Then he released my hand suddenly and with a big smile he said, 'Sit. You are tired. You are hungry. Sleep first and then have breakfast with me. We will eat bagels.' It took him less than a minute to extract me from the gutter in which I was wallowing. I sat down in the chair he pointed me towards and promptly fell asleep.

Three hours later, I opened my eyes to see the Rinpoche sitting in the same place, writing in a little book I had noticed in his hand when I arrived. Without turning to look at me, he called for Nicholas to present us with our bagels and we all sat together and ate in silence. When we finished, he said to me with a twinkle in his eye, 'They call me seven-bagel man here. I cannot eat one, I must eat seven in a day!' Then he laughed, delighted by a habit that gave him such unadulterated pleasure. I laughed with him as I visualized such a slight man devouring seven bagels. He looked at me, and he kept looking long after we stopped laughing, until I turned my eyes away.

Then he asked me to tell him what was troubling me. I told him I was sick, that I was an anorexic-bulimic. He didn't understand what it was and I had to explain it to him. He didn't asked me why and he didn't try to analyse me. He had taken my first words as my definition of myself, and though I was silently begging him to ask me more questions and engage with me, he didn't. Instead, he began reading from a book, but it was under his breath and it wasn't in English. I waited for what felt like an eternity, desperate for more dialogue, but there was none.

Finally, he looked up and asked, 'Do you have hope, Diya?'

I didn't respond; I was confused by the simplicity of the question and I was waiting for him to elaborate, but he didn't. The next time he spoke, just a few seconds later, he said, 'If you have hope, Diya, then you will be okay.'

SEVENTEEN

'Strong hope is a much greater stimulant of life than any single realized joy could be.'
– Friedrich Nietzsche

Against all odds I had found hope. It was inspired by my silent opposition to the ideology preached and methods used at PROMIS.

I simply refused to believe addiction could not be reversed and the pursuit of pleasure by an addict not be diseased by compulsion. I did not have the answer but I knew that, left open to interpretation, the twelve steps would guide me to the answer.

Melinda and Kenny were an illustration of the loose application of the label 'addict' and the mismanagement of the twelve-step programme. They were young, exploring life, and their lives so little lived could not be deemed unmanageable. They would have been better off in a juvenile detention centre, or some kind of correctional facility, rather than at PROMIS where they were being scrutinized and manacled by measures that were pre-emptive and had not been proven necessary.

I knew, albeit without certainty, that I would be okay,

even if after seventy-two excruciating hours my body
had not shown me any mercy. I was sitting in the lounge,
flanked by Melinda and Kenny, waiting for breakfast to
be announced. They were watching me as if I was the
key to their salvation, but all I had was hope. My body
continued to suffer, swollen with unrelinquished waste
and made taut by a pitiless struggle.

After a few minutes, Melinda asked me if I was quiet
because I was missing my cigarettes and coffee. Until she
asked me that question, I hadn't remembered either but
as soon as she voiced the sentiment, my willpower faltered
and I began to crave both.

I had avoided the pantry where patients were allowed
to help themselves to coffee and tea, and I had stopped
myself from venturing into the courtyard where the
smokers gathered for their nicotine fix. By sheer avoidance
I had managed to put mind over matter and escape my
habitual urges until they were prompted by Melinda.

I shut my eyes while Kenny screamed at her for
reminding me, and I fought to subdue my instinct to self-
destruct. Eventually I managed to recover my quietude
by repeating to myself the words of the serenity prayer,
turning over my will, once again, to that God which
remained a mystery to me.

As I contemplated how brittle the power of will is and
the control it generates, irrespective of who its keeper
might be, I was reminded of Confucius who wrote:

> *The will to win, the desire to succeed, the urge to reach your
> full potential ... These are the keys that will unlock the door
> to personal excellence.*

I had the will to win and the desire to succeed. What I did not possess was the right urge, and without all three instruments harmony was out of my reach; it was especially out of reach at PROMIS. I needed to feel it first and then think it. I was desperate to feel the power that was God but I didn't know how.

Jenna walked into the lounge to break up the fight between Melinda and Kenny, which had taken on belligerent tones and a thunderous volume. She stood before us with self-appointed authority, reprimanding the two teenagers and casting disapproving looks at me. She had assumed the role of headmistress in a pecking order developed by the patients, based either on their longevity at the treatment centre or on the degree of their surrender to the treatment.

Jenna's posture was risible in the context of a recovery center where people coexisted upon the admission that their lives had become unmanageable. But very subtly, control was being resurrected and roles assumed in what was a parallel world drained of our individual realities – those same realities had been destroyed by addiction and they had buried us in the rubble of their implosion.

Jenna's bullying tactics silenced Melinda and Kenny, but I wasn't about to be censored in that manner, nor was I going to allow Melinda and Kenny to be. I indicated to the two youngsters that breakfast had been announced, and as we walked towards the door of the lounge, I finally revealed myself. I stopped in front of Jenna, looked her straight in the eye and said, 'You are not in control here,

Jenna, and if you were in control at all, you wouldn't be here in the first place, so back off.'

She shook her head from side to side as I walked past having said what I needed to, but less than what I wanted to say to her and to the others. What Jenna chose to read in my response to her assault was brutish defiance, but as she sat down at the dining table opposite me, her insecurity was apparent.

I had seen Jennas all my life. I had tried to befriend them and their entourage which was constituted by people with worse insecurity and low self-esteem, people who shunned independence and individuality as if they were dirty words and ugly concepts. For most of my life I had done the same, in my desperation to belong. And in trying to find an anchor outside myself I had become estranged from the person I was at my core: that wide-eyed child full of curiosity and innocence, the one I ignored while I became a chameleon defined by an ever-changing environment and the people who passed through it. In the bargain, that child had become sick, and I realized that above and beyond all else, my duty was to her until she was cured.

As I observed the people around me, warped by their lives and caged by their definitions of themselves, I became convinced it was in that child that I would find pure instinct. I had to heal her and restore that instinct, but the medium of the intellect was not the right avenue, nor were the practices of the recovery centre which condemned her to permanent ill health. I glanced at Melinda and Kenny, who were sitting at a table adjacent to mine, and I winked at them. In spite of their misdemeanours, I could see their unspoilt youth steered by senses that were still vibrant. They were full of curiosity and spontaneity, and they were helping me find my way.

I had met many successful people in my life, and the ones engraved in my memory were those in possession of a childlike quality. That very quality was being desecrated at PROMIS, and when I tuned in to the voices around me, it was indisputable – Jenna was speaking volubly about the degree of her addiction and holding it up as a reference for the strength of her recovery. She was challenging the patients around her to compete with those statistics. It was woeful, the source of the identity she was trying to construct, like many of the other patients who competed on how much cocaine they had consumed, heroin they had injected and the depths of despair to which they had descended.

They were people who knew themselves only as addicts and they were not in search of greater knowledge. PROMIS was not for me and I would not, could not, find recovery there. I needed to return to my reality, but to do so I required the consent of my parents. I could only hope they would be able to see the charade and understand my resistance when they arrived.

I turned my attention to the plate of food before me, and to the wonders bestowed by the exercise of my sense of taste; it helped me eat without fear. Little did I know then that it was to become a powerful tool and one of my greatest talents – in complete opposition to the tenets of the recovery centre. PROMIS prescribed a regimented diet for all patients with an eating disorder, a diet motivated by need and devoid of desire. But I wanted to be like the Rinpoche. I wanted to be able to eat as many sesame-seed-studded bagels as I felt like, without conflict or compulsion. I wanted to feel the pleasure, or pain that lingers beyond the instant gratification which nourishes, punishes and sustains the addict's being.

I was walking a balance beam, but later that day, I began to sway in the right direction and the next morning my body finally succumbed to the laws of biology. It had been ninety-six hours, and I believe that was the day my instinct began to heal.

It was at the last group therapy session of the day that I reached my tipping point, elicited by a demonstration of dogmas which impelled me to passionately articulate my objection to the treatment programme. One of the patients, a glamorous lady named Bella who carried herself with a swagger, spoke of her command over the translation of recovery into her reality. She was a media celebrity, scheduled to return to London the following week with the blessings of the recovery centre.

She said she would have to renounce her swagger to protect her recovery, distance herself from friends with whom she had revelled in the abuse of alcohol and cocaine, arrange social engagements at different times of the day and in venues where alcohol was not served, attend open meetings of alcoholics and narcotics anonymous four times a week … And on she went, thinking her life out loud, planning, plugging, blaming, bandaging and, above all, calculating and controlling.

It was a soliloquy that gathered momentum as she gradually became as drugged by the powerful and all-protective illusion of her planned recovery as she had been by her addictions. Her performance held fortitude and courage but it was entirely bankrupt of conviction. It was an example of a controlled life engineered to evade choice and avoid sensibility, a replica of the life lived at PROMIS but without its brawny barricades and policemen.

It was in fact a different hue of that same deceitful high, the one destined for a dangerous fall.

On my first visit to the treatment centre I had quietly questioned if I would learn how to choose, and just a day earlier I had discovered I needed to let myself feel and learn how to negotiate those feelings. On my fourth day I was witness to the dismissal of both choice and sensibility as I watched the other patients and Robert nod in approval and give encouragement. They all but beat their chests by way of congratulating Bella, who might as well have been a victim of recovery, not a victor.

I was unable to restrain myself; I stood up and said, 'My god, you all need to be locked up and not in here. I cannot stomach this dishonesty. Robert, what the hell are any of us learning? Do you think your methods stand a chance against addiction when you don't teach us how to choose and how to stop fearing what we feel —'

I was cut off mid-sentence by Robert, who said, in a cunning tone, 'Well, this is a happy occasion, Diya. Finally you reveal your anger about being here and being an addict.'

I clenched my jaw and responded in a manner equally

sinuous. 'Oh, I am not angry about being here, Robert. I came here willingly and with blind faith. Mine is not anger; it is disappointment and disgust at your methods and manipulation of the twelve-step programme. You are not helping us, you are setting us up to fail.'

With those words I turned around and left the room. Behind me I heard the familiar chant, 'Thank you for sharing ...' this time addressed to Bella. There was a shuffle of chairs, and as I gained distance from the room, I heard a faint recital of the serenity prayer, in which I silently joined the others. But this time I asked for courage first, then wisdom and finally serenity:

God, grant me the courage to change the things I can, The wisdom to accept the things I cannot change, And serenity within me.

I had finally taken my own side.

EIGHTEEN

'Cry little one, just cry.'

On the morning of my fifth day at PROMIS, my instinct began to heal; my bodily functions were restored and my mind was freed, but with that freedom came the conflict of choice. I was suddenly frightened of leaving the centre, a place where twelve hours earlier, I had caught a glimpse of the person I was looking for – myself.

In a few hours, my parents would arrive and as I sat on the edge of my bed before going down to breakfast, I recollected the events of the previous day. I could not remember having thought about what I was going to say to Jenna, and what prompted my reaction to Bella and to the others in that room. I could not fathom what possessed me to stand boldly before the counsellor and challenge him, to turn on my heel, leave the room, and then revise the words of the serenity prayer in a way that felt right.

I shut my eyes and replayed those scenes in my mind. It was as if I had stepped out of myself and was watching a movie in slow motion. Later that evening, I refused to sit at the table reserved for patients with eating disorders. Instead, I took my pre-plated serving of food to the table occupied by Melinda and Kenny, and I watched them eat. They had served themselves what they liked, or what they least disliked and they ate with hunger until they were full. These were two feelings from which I was divorced – PROMIS neither offered any counselling nor a means of reconciliation.

As I ate my own food, playing a game of taste and texture to make 'the medicine go down', I felt, rather than thought, I had done the right thing. But in the morning my confidence was shaken.

For the first time in five days, I undressed in front of a full-length mirror and looked at myself. My reflection kept changing before my eyes – first I saw myself the same as when I arrived. Then I remembered having eaten and retained thirteen meals, and suddenly I saw myself much bigger than before. I shut my eyes and escaped the memory and when I opened them, I was the same, until my memory resurfaced once more, programmed by a sick instinct that saw obesity as the result of proper nourishment.

My instinct had only just begun to heal, its guidance treacherous. The removal of my bandages unharnessed a mind which had been a puppet on a string for several years, moving with the rhythm of addiction and intent of recovery. It continued to play tricks on me and I suspected it would be fragile outside the confines of PROMIS.

Fear enveloped me all over again, my internal dialogue a ruthless one, until I walked into the dining room that morning.

I looked around me and saw the same people occupy the same places at the same dining tables they had each and every day. They were guided by the habit and routine of recovery, just as they had been by the habit and routine of addiction. And suddenly, my decision was made: I was going to leave. What I didn't realize was just how hard it would be.

I was standing in the courtyard waiting for my parents, as the families and friends of other patients began to arrive. Melinda and Kenny stood with me, and I told them I planned to leave with my parents at the end of the day. I could see, by their forlorn expressions, that they felt let down. I tried to explain that it would help them if I could prove the flaws in the method of treatment and provide an alternative. Melinda looked at me, confused, and said, 'But what if you don't make it? What if you die like Henrietta?'

I put my arms around both her and Kenny and said, 'I won't die, I promise, and you have to promise me you won't do silly things when you leave – no drugs, no alcohol, nothing you have seen here from which people are suffering so terribly.'

They nodded in unison and we were all hugging one another when I heard the most beautiful sound in the world, the voice of my mother calling out to me. 'Lula,' she said, an abbreviation for Lula Mae, the pet name she had given me when I was a baby, as she held me in her arms outside the shop window of Tiffany's in New York City.

I turned around and ran towards my mother and father, all but dragging Melinda and Kenny with me. My father shook hands with them while my mother wrapped her arms around me. Then I hugged my father and he called me 'little one' as he pinched my cheek. The familiarity of his and my mother's greetings was more therapeutic than any method or medicine. It was with them that I would have a real chance of rediscovering the child they had brought into the world. All I needed was for them to take me home, but they didn't.

They said no, and I began to scream. It must have been shock that made me scream at the patients, counsellors, Melinda, Kenny and everyone standing in the courtyard when I heard my father say the words, 'No, we cannot take you with us. They have told us we must not.'

After lunch, the families and friends of the patients had attended a separate group therapy session convened by Alan, the head counsellor. In the course of the session, my parents were made to believe I was responding well to the treatment and that a premature end might be fatal to my well-being. Somehow, Alan had predicted I would attempt to terminate my treatment that day.

As I stood in the courtyard after my father's pronouncement, his words slaughtering my trust in him and my mother, all I could do was scream. I screamed that everyone at PROMIS was a freak, hell-bent on brainwashing our families and friends, and I continued to scream in rage and terror until Melinda grabbed my hand and pulled me towards the garden. She gently pushed me down onto the grass, and I remember feeling spent as I sat there, hugging my knees to my chest and staring straight ahead. A few moments later I asked Melinda to fetch me a cigarette. I hadn't smoked for sixty hours, but that child, the one I was trying to find and heal, had lost faith in me. And in that moment of defeat I turned to the only accessible addiction I had.

Melinda brought me a cigarette and sat down on the grass beside me while I smoked. She had no visitors that day. I put my arm around her protectively and we watched as Kenny spoke to my mother and father, his own parents trying to restrain him.

My mother came to me and I stood up; she put her hands on my shoulders and whispered in my ear, 'Find a way to come home. They said we are not to assist you, but if you really want to leave, you must find your own way home.' Then she gave Melinda a hug and told us to take care of each another.

Melinda looked at me with tears in her eyes. For the first time, since I had met her, she let down her guard – perhaps it was dismantled by that little bit of kindness from my mother. I took her in my arms, stroked her tiny head tenderly, and I said, 'Cry, little one, just cry.' Melinda cried until she could no more, then, recovering quickly, she raced off to find Kenny.

Kenny had tried to impress upon my parents that they should trust me; he told them I was strong, far stronger than the other patients and he asked them to let me find my own way.

Find my own way, find my own way – I kept repeating those same words to myself before I fell asleep that night. When I woke up the next morning I remembered the promise made to me by Paul six days earlier and I went to his office straight after breakfast.

'I have been expecting you, Diya,' he said.

I sat down opposite him and responded, 'Well, then you already know why I am here.'

Six days earlier, I had asked Paul to promise me that the day I wanted to leave he would drive me to Ashford station from where I would take the train back to Paris; and he had said, 'Yes, I promise.'

But as I sat across him, he wouldn't look me in the eye. I waited patiently until he said, 'Will you give it another five days? After five days if you still want to leave, I'll take you to Ashford.'

I said yes, and it was with a sense of relief. I felt comforted by the compromise; by the balance it brought to my conflicted mind, divided instinct and a will I no longer wished to exercise.

I had continued to smoke after my first cigarette the previous day, and earlier that morning I had returned to my habit of one-and-a-half mugs of coffee. I surrendered my will to my instinct with both fear and hope. I had to trust that my instinct, as it healed, would learn to drive my will once again, with fortified fuel and along a revised route.

Without realizing it, I had turned to steps two and three. I had come to believe I would find that power greater than myself, which could restore me to sanity, within my own instinct, retrained and released.

I sensed the journey I was about to take would have a perilous pulse and, as things turned out, it continued to fluctuate for a long time until I found my way to step eleven: to my conscious contact with God as I understood God.

For the next five days, I earnestly followed the routine

and practices of PROMIS. I was looking for anything that might assist me in my onward journey – but I found nothing that would help me rebuild a life without chains. Instead I recognized a fatal flaw in the treatment of anorexics – the twelve steps are built on the foundation of abstinence: a veritable death sentence for any person suffering from anorexia nervosa.

On the eleventh day I packed the little bag I had brought with me and readied myself to leave the centre after attending the first group therapy session. I was standing in the courtyard, smoking a cigarette, when Alan found me and asked me to join him in the lounge. He had already denied me his blessings on the eve of my departure – what I didn't expect was to receive a curse.

Inside the lounge, Alan asked me, innocently, what I was going to do and how I planned to pursue and protect my recovery. I answered that my plan was simply to surrender control and teach myself to feel my way through – a practice PROMIS appeared to contradict, at times even forget, in their application of the twelve step programme as a method of treatment.

But Alan was far more intelligent than me; he quoted Albert Einstein, by way of rebuttal, his tone tinged with a subtle warning when he said, 'We should take care not to make the intellect our God.'

I laughed nervously and informed him I had nothing further to say. Then I thanked him and held out my hand to shake his, but he refused it. 'Okay then.' I said, shrugged and turned to leave when I heard him say, 'You are going to die, Diya.'

I stopped in my tracks, disabled by a proclamation that was nothing short of poisonous. I stood still, my back to Alan, until my fists involuntarily curled and uncurled, my hands began to shake and my mouth quivered. Then I turned and said in a tone more threatening than any I had ever used in my life. 'No, Alan I am going to survive and I am going to live a life you cannot even dream of. You, Alan, are not my God. Fuck you.'

I walked out of the lounge, picked up my bag and went straight to Paul. I asked him to take me to the station at once. I did not attend the group therapy session nor did I say my goodbyes. I managed to catch an earlier train to Paris and when I was finally in my seat, I put my arms around myself and whispered, 'Cry, little one, just cry.'

I cried into my own arms – arms I had never lent myself before that day.

NINETEEN

Recovery-relapse-regret-reform …
Recovery-relapse-regret-reform …

I was going home; not to Paris, not to Number 2 rue du General Lambert, the residence of the Indian ambassador to France, not to the wood-panelled bedroom I called my own. I was going home to my mother and father, their presence the only constant in my life.

As I approached the Eiffel Tower in a taxi, I asked the driver to stop at the corner of Le Pont d'Iena, a beautiful bridge across the River Seine, between the Eiffel Tower and the Trocadero. The sun was shining in a bright blue sky and I decided to walk the rest of the way, just a few hundred metres.

I hadn't had the chance to telephone my mother and tell her I was on an earlier train, so I took a taxi from the Gare du Nord station, relishing every moment of my freedom from scrutiny. But I was scared, I was scared of being scared and I was scared of my parents being scared.

My mother had sounded anxious on the telephone when I spoke to her from Paul's office to tell her I was coming home. She asked me about which groceries were to have stocked, special dishes to be prepared, whether I would like my meals to be served at the same times as at the recovery centre ... Endless questions bursting with fear and hope. I felt choked as I answered, with artificial confidence, that it was okay, everything would be okay and she didn't need to recreate the same meal plan as the one imposed on me at PROMIS.

I didn't know how to explain to her that what I needed was to learn how to eat, to learn how to choose and to feel my way through. Yet I understood her fear, for it reflected my own – that fear turned out to be the most dangerous weapon against recovery. It is a powerful magnet to the circle of relapse, regret, reform and recovery, not only for an addict but for any person who wills change and fears its failure; a fear I had always shouldered.

I entered the house through the service entrance, operated by an electronic lock and an entry code. It was a four-digit code I had often forgotten or been unable to punch in properly when I came home at night, drunk and unsteady on my feet, with eyes I couldn't focus and fingers which trembled uncontrollably.

I was flooded by memories of my misconduct, and it took all my energy and recital of the serenity prayer to help restore my equilibrium. I shut the door behind me and called out 'hello'.

The first person I saw was our cook Joseph; he had worked for us since I was nine years old. He hurried up the stairs from the basement kitchen to take my bag from me. His eyes were glazed with tears and he touched my arm tentatively, as if to evaluate proof of my presence and well-being. I took his hand in mine as he called out to my mother.

It was the first time I had held Joseph's hand in such a manner. Suddenly I wanted to express to him my gratitude for his presence in my life. Like so much else, it was something I had taken for granted while I lived in those trenches of my being where my senses had been smothered. Just one month earlier, it was Joseph who had opened the door to the bathroom and lifted me from a pool of vomit. I gripped his hand tightly to try and convey my reassurance that it would never happen again. It did, but Joseph was spared.

I walked into the palatial lobby of the house and saw my mother walking down the grand staircase. She was followed by my brother and I almost whooped with joy when I caught sight of him; Vivan had never treated me like an addict, a sick person. We continued to communicate with each other the same way we had as children, both naughty and carefree. He made me laugh, really laugh, like the Rinpoche had done in New York City. It must be one of the most liberating expressions, more powerful than any drug-induced high.

Some years later, after I had relocated to New Delhi, I discovered something known as laughter meditation at the park in front of my house. Every morning a group of people gathered there to laugh together, at nothing at all, as loudly as they could, until they spent all the tears that infected them with illness of mind or body.

The day I went home, Vivan helped me make the transition back to my reality and, some years later, he proved to be the final trigger that effected my evolution from an addict in recovery to a recovered human being.

When my father came home that evening, we had a joyful reunion ... Until dinner was served. It comprised roast chicken, French beans, baked potatoes and a green salad. Just as I was about to serve myself, my mother and father began arguing about portioning my food – and I stumbled. Suddenly I didn't know what to eat and how much to eat. Their argument had shattered the delicate connection between my mind and instinct; I struggled to feel my appetite, to do the right thing, not only to pacify them but also appease my own guilt.

They were doing exactly what the counsellors at PROMIS had told them to not do – they were meant to let go, to surrender their roles as my policemen, but it was just as hard for them as it was for me.

They watched me closely, despite Vivan's attempts to distract them, and I felt grateful for my sense of taste in which I submerged myself as I ate. It helped arrest the duality that was back at a tipping point – I was fearful but I had also found hope, and I had to preserve the duality until my instinct found the power to choose, to be singular rather than plural.

That night I went to sleep tortured by the internal conflict between me and I. 'I' was no longer defined, neither by addiction nor by the intent to recover, and 'me' was trying to emerge from the chamber in which it had been buried.

An ordinary life for me at the age of twenty-three would have comprised a job and a circle of friends, but I had neither. All I had was a blank canvas on which I felt an urgency to start drawing.

The next day, Vivan returned to London; he worked as a trader for the investment bank Salomon Bros, and in England he enjoyed friendships cemented over the many years of his life there. It was a life I envied, and soon I found myself leapfrogging into the same life – except, I was vastly unprepared for it. I ran before I learned how to walk, and I ran straight into relapse, followed by regret, then reform and finally recovery all over again.

I had contested the practices of PROMIS and I had told others and myself I would find my own way. But I tumbled into life like a willful child, hurting myself repeatedly, bandaging and unbandaging myself until I was raw.

Much later I discovered it is only through an exploration of the senses that a self develops in which there is no duel or duality. We then realize the home we all crave, the one that both anchors us and travels with us, is the one we find inside ourselves.

But my home lay in my mother and father and the next day when they announced they wanted to take me with them on a holiday to the south of France, I said yes. I should have said no. I was scared of being left to my own devices and my disloyalty to myself led me towards my first relapse: always the most painful one.

We were at the summer home of one of the publishing magnates of France in the beautiful town of La Croix Valmer, near Saint Tropez on the Côte d'azur. It was a majestic seafront estate, where we stayed for four days.

Amongst the other guests there was a Mr Gilles Weil, then vice-president of the giant cosmetics company, L'Oreal. It was a glamorous setting and a harsh contrast to the one I had just surfaced from, divested of my defences and many bandages.

For four days the guests were required to dress for breakfast, lunch and dinner. Every gathering was a celebration of garb and gastronomy, at which both costume and excess were in order. I had carried a suitable wardrobe with me but I hadn't realized I had outgrown much of it. For nearly two weeks, I had worn clothes that shielded me from weight gain, but when I dressed for my first evening at the estate, the garments which had earlier ballooned around my tiny frame, hugged me uncomfortably. And I betrayed myself. I was no longer able to hide from the increase in weight, my Achilles heel, confronted with which my duality tipped from hope to fear.

I reached out for the only pair of crutches I could access: I ate more than I could retain, I drank copiously to find both courage and a connection with the others and I purged myself three times a day for the next four days – I had not been ready to present myself to the world. Instead I revived one of the many personalities I had fabricated, with which I charmed, intrigued and held my audience while I hurt and abandoned myself all over again.

My mother knew I was in the throes of a relapse, but she decided to withdraw just as she had been advised. I turned to the serenity prayer, my only solace, and I apologized to the child within me; I asked her for forgiveness and to have patience.

When we returned to Paris, I managed to resume recovery, restore and retain nourishment and remove alcohol from my diet. I began to exercise to help counter the weight gain, but it was frenzied and felt like punishment to a body crying out for a little bit of kindness and a lot of rest. I could not lose the weight, which must have been no more than 3 kg. I was too frightened to weigh myself, to cede control and have faith in my journey to freedom from addiction.

I began to eat less and less and before I knew it, I was back on a merry-go-round that fractured the fragile relationship I had forged with myself ... Eventually I was thrown off, an exit so savage I had nothing left to fear.

It all began with an offer of employment from L'Oreal Paris, the initiative taken by the vice-president Mr Gilles Weil. Such was my misguided intent to prove PROMIS wrong and live my life according to the same standards as everyone else that I didn't look before I leapt. Those standards proved to be not only premature, but also punitive for the child I was trying to heal.

While we were in the south of France, it was decided that, on my return to Paris, I would be interviewed by HR, L'Oreal as a mere formality. I hastily joined the company and shortly afterwards, my father received notice of his retirement. He, my mother, Joseph, the rest of the staff and our little family of dogs were to return to India three months later.

It was too late for me to withdraw from the life I had plunged into – a life that gave the false appearance of health and prosperity so long as I had the refuge I called my home.

I had been manipulating my recovery with strict control over an inadequate diet and a rigorous exercise regime, while my job gave me a feeling of purpose and temporary reprieve from a punishing routine. I had managed to deceive myself into believing I had found my own way and my freedom from addiction.

But the day my family left is the day I began the real battle between me and I – it was a vicious fight to the finish line and marked a brand new beginning of my life.

TWENTY

… It matters not how strait the gait,
How charged with punishments the scroll
I am the master of my fate:
I am the captain of my soul.
— William Ernest Henley

I changed two words in the last verse of the poem 'Invictus' – Unconquered – a poem recited by Nelson Mandela each and every day of his imprisonment on Robben Island.

Like a prayer, I would say it as often as I could, but I said 'you', not 'I': I addressed the child inside me. She was the master of my fate, the captain of my soul, and I was trying to find my way back to her.

Everything conspired to prevent that from happening. It is, I believe, the same kind of conspiracy many human beings have to contend with in their lives: we keep being distanced from ourselves in our search for a lasting place in a world that is continuously changing. And as we try to keep pace and secure our positions, we not only bribe our souls but also contort our personalities until we become unrecognizable.

My time at PROMIS recovery center taught me to detect that conspiracy; what I had to learn was how to disassemble it.

I moved out of the residence of the Indian ambassador and into a studio apartment on a cobbled street called La rue des Lombards, in the 1st district of Paris. It was as modest a location as its predecessor had been grand. My parents objected to my new habitat but I felt more comfortable than I had in the 7th district of Paris – there my environment had commanded both costume and conduct that adulterated rather than adorned my being. The little studio was snug and manageable. The absence of prestige did not embarrass me as I climbed out of the official car of the Ambassador for the very last time; it deposited me just outside my apartment after I had seen my parents off at Charles de Gaulle Airport.

The pomp and ceremony of their farewell by embassy personnel and other local dignitaries had demanded a stoic posture of me, but I was unable to contain myself when I said goodbye to our little family of dogs. Their infrangible faith in me was a potent pill for perseverance on that dreaded day.

When I entered my studio, I clasped my hands, held them against my abdomen and recited the last verse of the poem 'Invictus'. The words kept hope alive while fear carried me, once again, into the soul destroying sequence of relapse, regret, reform and recovery.

I felt empty and alone, two feelings for which my tried and tested antidote was the abuse of food and alcohol. Joseph had stocked the studio kitchenette with all the essentials: milk, wholewheat bread, Weetabix cereal, bananas, eggs, Marmite and an assortment of vegetables. I didn't know how to cook, not even how to boil an egg. I reached for the box of cereal and proceeded to assemble the only meal I knew how to – breakfast, at what was dinner time – but it did little to quench the emptiness and hamper my loneliness.

My very fear of those feelings catapulted me from my studio onto the streets; I wandered without purpose or destination until I found myself sitting down at a table on the terrace of a café-bar.

I ordered a carafe of the house red wine and a robust meal I knew I would not retain. It was the month of March in 1998, the chill of winter still in the air, encouraging my request for a 'Coq au Vin': it is a rustic winter dish, originally from Burgundy, constituted by chicken braised in red wine and garnished with pearl onions, bacon and mushrooms.

The wine arrived, accompanied by a basket of warm crusty baguette and a bowl of Normandy butter, the custom of every French eating house. I poured myself a large glass of wine and drank greedily, until I felt my fear dilute. Then I turned my attention to the Coq au Vin perched on a bed of mashed potatoes, served just a few moments earlier.

I began to eat and I tasted everything I ate. Gradually I became intoxicated by the nuance of cooked wine, reduced to an almost sweet syrup, the earthiness of charred mushrooms, the smoky bouquet released by seared bacon, the buttery texture of chicken that fell from the bone and the silky mashed potato which absorbed all the flavours and completed the dish.

My game of taste consumed me and it helped vaccinate the child inside me against the addiction.

That night I returned to my studio and vomited– but my addiction had been stripped of the high produced by purging myself of nourishment– I felt no relief, only regret. So I sat on bended knees and I prayed:

God, grant me the courage to change the things I can,
The wisdom to accept the things I cannot change
And serenity within.
It matters not how strait the gait,
How charged with punishments the scroll
You are the master of my fate:
You are the captain of my soul.

The next day, and every day after that, I woke up in the morning to a powerful promise of reform, followed by that familiar breakfast of Weetabix, toast with Marmite and a banana; it was a meal I could easily assimilate.

For the first time, I went to work by public transport. I was an assistant product manager at Lancôme, one of the prestigious brands under the umbrella of L'Oréal, headquartered in a suburb of Paris to which I had to commute by subway and bus.

I felt a sense of achievement in the transition I made from a privileged to a pedestrian life, but my achievement was oppressed by the imprisonment I felt in a job that went against my grain. I was not interested in the world of beauty and cosmetics. The superficiality nauseated me, especially when I watched my colleagues wear their employment by Lancôme as an emblem of elegance and a symbol of superiority.

I was placed in charge of a new skin-whitening cream, destined for consumers in India and Japan. I found it unthinkable that people could disfigure themselves out of choice, mask and masquerade themselves with pleasure, when, in my life, such practices represented a poison that produced so much pain. But I had made my bed and was forced to lie in it until I found a way forward into the life that was meant to be mine.

In the first few weeks after my parents' departure, I kept to myself as much as I could. I was not ready to revive the company of friends and acquaintances – it required great effort for me to perform the various personalities I had tailor-made for each one of them, and I felt tired as I adjusted to my new routine. I was forced to reserve my stamina, to be able to fulfil reform and recovery after each episode of relapse and regret.

Eventually, when the loneliness became overbearing, I retrieved my costumes and masks, and I reached out to those happy to accompany me in my exploration of food and wine. It was a covert education I was unconsciously giving myself, the fruit of which was an expertise in gastronomy I would one day exploit the same way I had allowed food and alcohol to exploit me.

But very soon, I found myself back on that merry-go-round which slowly gathered speed … I tripped into a social whirlpool that took me beyond the benign abuse of my body in bars and restaurants to aggressive abuse at dinner parties, dance parties, weekends at the estates of young aristocrats, holidays in Sicily, Budapest, New York … Until I was physically unable to withstand any more. My body was battered by excess and expulsion, my rational mind ripped apart and hollow, in which the only echo was of my recital of the poem 'Invictus'.

> *Out of the night that covers me*
> *Black as the pit from pole to pole,*
> *I thank whatever gods may be*
> *For my unconquerable soul.*
>
> *In the fell clutch of circumstance*
> *I have not winced nor cried aloud.*
> *Under the bludgeonings of chance*
> *My head is bloody, but unbowed.*
>
> *Beyond this place of wrath and tears*
> *Looms but the Horror of the shade,*
> *And yet the menace of the years*
> *Finds, and shall find, me unafraid.*
>
> *It matters not how strait the gate,*
> *How charged with punishments the scroll.*
> *YOU are the master of my fate:*
> *YOU are the captain of my soul.*

I put in my resignation at L'Oreal after seven months of employment in which I had hardly been present. I was disengaged from both my work and colleagues, exhausted by a life of late nights and dazed by hangovers and malnourishment. The company was not sad to see me go. My resignation was received without any hesitation or imposition of a notice period. I was free to leave with immediate effect. All I had left to do was tell my parents I was coming home. I had failed to find my own way – but I was not going to admit defeat.

A few months earlier, at a dinner party held in the home of the Hottinguer family, owners of the prestigious private bank, I had met two well-known American men in their early seventies; each one had a significant influence on my next steps. They were Dominic Dunne, author and investigative journalist, and Robert Denning, interior decorator for the rich and famous.

Shortly afterwards, I travelled to New York City for a weekend of rigorous revelry. On my last evening there I was invited by Dominic to dine with him at Mortimer's on Lexington avenue, a virtual private club for the elite. It is an evening that remains precious in my memory, during which Dominic told me a story. That story supported my theory on freedom, not only from addiction but also recovery. The story was his.

Dominic was a recovered addict who no longer used the crutch of the twelve-step programme. He said, at first, the programme had limited him, but when it furtively began to imprison him, he knew he had to break away.

I could see he was a man who had found both peace and friendship with himself. He was sure of who he was as he introduced me to the movers and shakers in the restaurant that evening – Bill Blass, Nan Kempner and other well known personalities. He moved with ease between them and me, a person with no credentials whatsoever. He offered me wine to drink, comfortable with his own abstinence, and he spoke of his most prized possession, his freedom from both addiction and the prison of recovery.

That day Dominic instilled faith in me even while I lay in the furrows of failure, and back in Paris, it was Robert Denning who lifted me onto the next leg of my journey.

I was at a bar called Le Fumoir – a late-night cigar and martini bar adjacent to the Louvre museum – and I was sipping a brandy that scalded my stomach. A few weeks earlier, I had begun to spew blood whenever I vomited and occasionally when I coughed, but I could neither stop drinking nor vomiting. Instead I had become immune to the pain generated by my ingestion of food and alcohol.

That night, after dinner with Robert and a young friend of his, Lowell Liebermann, an American composer, conductor and pianist, we went to Le Fumoir to continue an evening of voluble introspection and exchange.

Robert was staring at me as I laughed with Lowell about the time he had met my parents in Monaco and how charmed and intimidated he had been by them. I was revelling in his company when Robert suddenly interrupted us – he looked at me almost threateningly and said, 'Diya, you are wasting yourself at L'Oreal, in the corporate world. You are a creative person and you must find your calling.'

Lowell joined forces with him, both men able to see something in me I couldn't see in myself. Others had seen it too, but they had been unable to elucidate what it was.

Robert went a step further and made me an offer I couldn't refuse, an offer that would take me home to my parents. Neither Robert nor Lowell knew how sick I was.

Two days later, I put in my resignation at L'Oreal. I cleared my office of all my personal belongings and I returned to my studio where I sat in silence for a long time, staring at my mobile telephone. Finally I called my mother; I told her I was coming home for a change in career, in collaboration with Robert Denning, one of the most famous interior decorators in New York City.

Robert had advised me to return to India and look for a cost-effective way of developing twenty colour prints on silk taffeta; he was trying to find a cheaper alternative to those he was importing to the United States from Italy, and he gave me both direction and instruction in how to proceed.

I was excited by the prospect but I could feel that I was not able. My physical disrepair gnawed at me relentlessly while I spoke to my mother – and I knew I was telling her a lie.

I was going home to my parents, to New Delhi, India, but I was going towards a fall, not a rise from the ashes.

TWENTY-ONE

'Keep your friends close and your enemies closer.'
– Sun Tzu, 'The Art of War'

The airplane touched down in New Delhi, India, the country of which I was a citizen and where I arrived a virtual corpse.

Joseph was at the airport to receive me and the moment I saw him, I knew there was much more at stake than my own dissolution. On this occasion, his eyes were not glazed with tears of relief; they were arid, lifeless, and he greeted me with a smile that did not reach his eyes.

I could not return the smile. In broken Hindi, I said to him, 'Tell me.'

My mother was bedridden with a herniated disc in her spine, three of our dogs had died of illness and old age in the seven months I had been absent, and my father and mother had decided to divorce.

A dam of emotion burst as Joseph spoke and he allowed himself to cry in the comfort of my presence. But the pain he shed, I absorbed, and it opened the gates of hell for me.

My worst fears had been realized and they drove the final arrow into a heart that was already bleeding.

Once I was in the car, on my way to a home that was disintegrating, I began to writhe in agony. I felt an acute pain puncture my abdomen and provoke acid reflux that flooded my mouth with bloody bile, blood I could taste and had to swallow.

I told Joseph I felt terribly sick and that I needed to go to a hospital as soon as possible. I wanted to spare my parents but Joseph was helpless. I was forced to go home first, to face the wreckage of a home in which I had an incapacitated mother, a father dethroned of his position as head of a united family and nothing but the memory of three precious pets.

It was a bitter-sweet reunion fraught with fear. Tentatively, I embraced my father at the entrance of a penthouse apartment in a suburb of New Delhi. Joseph told him I had to be taken to a hospital immediately, his announcement made unnecessary when I stumbled in pain as I leaned down to greet our two little dogs. At first they wagged their tails and licked my face, which had begun to perspire heavily. Then they ran towards the room in which my mother lay, turned around and barked at me to follow them.

I limped along a narrow corridor of the apartment, just as Henrietta had limped, one year earlier, across the courtyard of PROMIS recovery centre – but the difference was that I wanted to survive, and I wanted it more than ever when I reunited with my mother. She was the mother of the child I had tortured and in her eyes, that day, I saw not only renunciation but also deep sorrow at the way in which I had violated myself.

My father made the necessary arrangements at a hospital next door, and just as I was about to leave my mother's side, I said to her: 'I am going to be fine, mummy, do not worry.' I had never before given her my re-assurance.

An hour later, I was lying in fetal position on a hospital bed, waiting to be given an endoscopy. When the nurse offered me an anaesthetic, I refused – I wanted to feel the pain, I no longer wanted to escape it. And not only did I feel the pain, I also saw the damage I had done in blood-red.

As soon as the tube entered my oesophagus, I began to choke; with each gasp, blood surged from my mouth and onto my chest, the hospital gown, my shoulder and everywhere I looked. I began to shake my head in panic and the doctor held my hand and squeezed – he told me the procedure was nearly over and I would be okay. I looked at him and kept looking at him as I felt my fear right through to the end.

I had bleeding ulcers all over my duodenum and I was immediately admitted to the hospital and put on an intravenous drip through which I was medicated, nourished and sedated. My father stayed with me until I was ready to sleep and when he left, I looked down at my abdomen and said, 'I am sorry. I am so, so sorry.'

For the next three weeks, I remained in the hospital, and as I healed, so did my mother. She and I were to move into a small apartment above my grandparent's home, and I realized then, I had nothing left to fear.

While I was hospitalized, I tried to recall all the feelings that had threatened me – I forced myself to feel loneliness, emptiness, anger and sorrow until each one systematically dissolved and the hope I harboured rose to the surface, unfettered by fear. But I had to find a mechanism to sustain the non-duality – fragile in the face of life's many challenges – another lesson I had learned the hard way after I left PROMIS.

The search for that mechanism is what defined me for the next one year; it was a search that brought me not only recovery but also freedom from recovery, and a life in which I finally met myself.

In my last week at the hospital, I was gently rehabilitated. I was taken for walks on the grounds of the hospital and the intravenous feeding was replaced by a soft diet of clear vegetable soup and mashed potatoes. It was a diet I was prescribed for six weeks and I followed it religiously until the day I met an Ayurvedic physician. He followed a system of traditional Indian medicine based on the biological energies of the body that affect both the physical and mental processes.

One of the nurses at the hospital had advised me to seek the help of Ayurveda to learn how to eat again. She was an older woman with a daughter my age and her advice, soaked in empathy, introduced me to a world in which the rational mind is silenced and instinct cleansed. The day I was discharged, I thanked her repeatedly, as if to make up for all the gratitude I had never before expressed – to Sunil Chakraborty, Nicholas, Dominic, Robert, the Rinpoche, Henrietta, Melinda, Kenny … And most importantly, my mother, father and brother who are the real heroes of my story.

My father took me home, to a new home where I went to live with my mother and our two dogs. But that day I began to feel my real home, the one inside me, where I would always be with both my mother and father.

Some weeks later, in the newspapers, I read about an Ayurvedic treatment centre called Kairali and I went there for a consultation. I took all my medical reports with me but the physician showed no interest in reading them. Instead, he felt my pulse, examined my tongue, then my eyes and with just that brief examination he diagnosed my body and mind. He told me that my constitution was dominated by the energies of space and air – vata – but with a strong influence of the energy of fire – pitta. He said both energies were extreme in me, they were damaging me and must be neutralized. It was fascinating, the way he went on to describe my mind and spirit, derived from his diagnosis of the sickness in my body: a veracious account of the state of my being.

He prescribed a two-week treatment of a specific Ayurvedic oil massage and a diet rich in heavy, yet healthy foods: butter, cottage cheese, ghee, pine nuts … All to be consumed without any chilli and little spice. The diet was designed to pacify the energy of fire and subdue the energy of air. That day I went home with a spring in my step, still a weak step as my ulcerated body continued to heal, but the next day, when the treatment began and I changed my diet, the magic unfolded.

At first I was frightened of including those foods in my diet, but I incorporated them in a measured way – only once a day, at dinner time. Over the next two weeks, my body became leaner and more muscular than it had ever been. I would wake early, bursting with an energy I had not felt for nine years, in which each morning had been marred by my aching head, listless body and mind in distress.

Every afternoon without fail, I went to the center for my treatment. I lay naked on a wooden bed while two ladies massaged the length and breadth of my body with medicated oils. But it was when they stroked my abdomen, in a gentle circular motion, that I felt a healing I cannot explain. I cried, I laughed, I shivered, I fell asleep and then woke up, I felt emptied, then filled, and when it was over, I left the centre feeling lighter, more alive and alert than I had ever felt before.

When the two-week treatment ended, the Ayurvedic doctor asked me to attend a three-day course called the 'Art of Living'. He said to me, 'You need more healing; you need to learn how to breathe.' And that was when I discovered the power of the breath – it generated a high, levitation above consciousness unlike anything I had ever known.

For three days I followed and learned a technique of breathing called 'sudarshankriya', in addition to the basic movements of yoga that aligned the body. Together, they produced a harmony in the rhythm of my mind, body and breath, enkindling a joy that was entirely uncompromised. When the course ended, I began to feel, to really feel.

For the first time in my life, I felt my way through a day and I was able to trust my feelings. I felt what I wanted and needed to do in a day and I felt my thoughts.

I had at last stumbled upon step eleven; I had found God in my instinct, and as I continued to heal, that instinct guided me to a professor of yoga and a real-life philosopher: Sanjeev Bhanot.

I was searching for a more profound connection with myself, with that child inside me – the day I met Sanjeev, he told me he could give me what I wanted. All I had to do was make a commitment to him of six weeks. He asked me to come to him every morning, to study and practise yoga – to cement a new relationship with myself. He showed me how to befriend my body and allow my body to steer my mind.

Sanjeev took me through rigorous duality: he made me do asanas that produced pleasure until they caused pain, that lifted me high on hope and then dropped me in fear, that made me laugh abundantly and then cry, that allowed me to breathe in life and then suffocate myself. When he let go, I did the asanas on my own, bringing myself only pleasure and no pain, only laughter and no tears, only hope and no fear, and finally, a fluid breath.

Suddenly I felt strong and self-reliant. But when those six weeks were over and it was time for me to go on my way, I was frightened all over again; I was frightened of leaving Sanjeev. He asked me to come to him the following morning at sunrise. In his studio he made me do thirteen rounds of Surya namaskar: I was made to perform each sequence of twelve asanas with only one inhalation at the beginning and an exhalation at the end.

When I finished what felt like the roller-coaster ride of a lifetime, I stood before him and I felt fearless. He took

my hands in his and told me I was ready to stand on my
own two feet, to walk my way to the life waiting for me –
the one that was meant to be mine.

But I still had one battle left to win, and I was finally
prepared to fight it.

I had been secretly studying the different principles of
nutrition and I was immersed in control of my diet: how
much I ate, when I ate and what combinations of food I
ate. I was, in fact, following the same ordered system of
recovery as at PROMIS, in which food was treated as an
unassailable enemy, and hunger and satiety denied.

I had kept myself safe. I did not go out to eat and I
always ate on my own, only occasionally with my mother
and father. I had not made any friends, nor did I want
to, while I nurtured myself and sheltered my recovery.
Instead, I spent hours researching gastronomy, recalling
the dishes and flavours I had tasted in the many countries
in which I had lived. My curiosity was insatiable and my
passion unparalleled.

Then one day, while I was at home with my mother
and father, their continued friendship one in which I
luxuriated, my father said to me, 'You seem to know so
much about food and you appear to be equally fascinated
by it, but little one, how about learning how to cook?'

I looked at him wide-eyed, the idea intimidating yet
irresistible. Instinctively I said, 'Yes, you are right; I need
to learn how to cook. I want to.'

I had heard of a school in London called Le Cordon
Bleu, considered to be one of the best in the world for
culinary training in the techniques of French and other

European cuisines. There were schools elsewhere, but on many occasions, my brother, who lived in London, had asked me to come and stay with him; he felt I had become a prisoner of myself in my time of recovery.

That night I went onto the Internet to read about Le Cordon Bleu, London, a school from which I would graduate with an expertise in the culinary arts. But as I continued to read about the rigorous schedule in which I would have to live, breathe and taste all types of food each and every day, I realized it posed a very real threat to my recovery.

I sat quietly for a while, contemplating my choices, but I felt unable to make a decision. I was in a cage to which the key lay at arm's length and I couldn't reach for it. Finally when I got into bed and shut my eyes, I heard a voice inside me say: 'Keep your friends close and your enemies closer.'

The following morning, I applied for a seat at Le Cordon Bleu London.

TWENTY-TWO

'To win without risk is to triumph without glory.'
– Pierre Corneille

Number 27, Neal Street, Covent Garden, London WC2H
9PA was my new address, but it wasn't home; my home
was one that I guarded carefully inside me.

I was going to live with my brother while I attended
cooking school and I remember feeling fiercely protective
of myself as I made my way to Covent Garden.

No. 27 was a four-storey house on a pedestrian street,
the living area a glass-ceilinged room that opened into a
small patio overlooking the rooftops of Covent Garden.

I must have resembled Eliza Doolittle when I arrived.
I was filled with both excitement and apprehension, as if I
already knew I was about to go through a metamorphosis.
But it was a transformation that proved to be so painful, I
very nearly gave up.

Vivan never let me. His words, some of the most
important ever said to me, were 'back yourself Diya, for
once in your life, just back yourself'.

On my first morning in London, a city in which I was a
stranger all over again, I found myself faced with a tough

challenge. I had to go to a supermarket to buy groceries for myself. I was desperate to adhere to the system of nourishment I had established, and as I stood in one of the aisles of Marks & Spencer's supermarket, I felt paralysed.

There was no Marmite, no Weetabix, and I realized I had no idea how to shop in a supermarket. I was twenty-six years old and I didn't know how to buy groceries, how to cook or how to eat.

I wandered the aisles for a long time, trying to remember my lessons in nutrition and the foods that were safe for me to eat. Eventually I managed to locate a basket in which I gathered some wholewheat bread, olive oil, almonds, cottage cheese, beetroot and apples. I went home with a sense of accomplishment, promptly mutilated by my brother when he looked inside my shopping bags, hoping to find something for himself. His was a bachelor lifestyle, and he lived on his whims and fancies without any formula, only flair.

His face twisted in horror and he asked me if that was all I ate in a day. I answered stubbornly, even though I stammered when I said, 'Yes, it's enough for me.'

He withdrew while I ate a plain toast and some almonds. After I had finished eating, he told me he was going to take me to Le Cordon Bleu in the afternoon to make my payments and collect my school uniform and equipment. Then he informed me that I was to have dinner with him and his friends; I had met many of them in the past when I visited Vivan in Cambridge.

I smiled an artificial smile of gratitude even while that sinking feeling of fear overcame me once again. I had neither been to a restaurant nor interacted with people my own age for a very long time. I lay down in bed, struck by jetlag, and I let my fear take its course until it corroded. But it came back again and again, challenging and testing me each time with greater fervour.

That afternoon, I shivered as I walked out of Le Cordon Bleu cooking school, located just off Marylebone High Street. While Vivan had dealt with the administrative work, I observed the people around me, chefs and students, both sure-footed and strong. They wore an air of expertise and professionalism that cremated the confidence with which I had come – confidence I had built and managed to sustain in that home inside me where I had become a prisoner.

I had not allowed anyone in for a long time and I had not let the undulating rhythm of life creep in either. I was about to break out of that prison and when I did, all my preconceived notions of who I was crumbled, while the foundations of my home were left untouched.

I followed Vivan into a restaurant-bar called The Oriel, located on Sloane Square, and I let my fear penetrate but not poison me. I wore no masks and, timorously, I greeted his friends, their exuberance overwhelming. I sat quietly on a chair and tried to listen to the chatter while waves of panic rose and fell within me.

Vivan offered me a glass of wine, which I refused vehemently. Then I recoiled, feeling injured by his offer. I hadn't touched alcohol in over a year and I had avoided any circumstance in which I would have had to make the choice of whether or not to drink.

I sat there, feeling threatened, and then tortured when I was presented with the dinner menu. Suddenly, there were a hundred voices in my head and I could neither think nor hear. I looked up and saw Vivan and his friends pointing at the menu, talking to and laughing with one other, gesturing at the waiter … I shut my eyes and let the panic subside.

When I opened them again, the waiter was standing beside me waiting for my order. I looked at the menu and very slowly and deliberately I asked for a starter: the goat's cheese and caramelized onion tart. Then, diffidently, I added a glass of red wine to the order.

It was a dish I had eaten many times in Paris, each time accompanied by wine, but I had never digested either. And in the past year, I had not permitted myself to eat any cheese or white flour. That evening, when I placed my order, I took a small step towards unlocking the door of my prison of recovery.

The wine arrived before the food, and after my very first sip, there was a rush of blood to my brain, a repositioning of that high which alters both mind and body. I began to fight it with a fury. I didn't want to be high; I wanted to taste the wine, enjoy the way it complemented the melting cheese of my tart, and the flaky puff pastry case in which the onions had been caramelized to a subtle sweetness – new sensations that unfurled like poetry on my palate.

I deafened myself to the noise around me. I ate slowly and I concentrated on the tastes and textures swarming my mouth. I didn't speak to anyone and I didn't hear anyone speak. Instead I tried to exercise mindfulness, a practice to which I had been introduced in a book written by a Vietnamese Zen Buddhist monk, Thich Nhat Hanh, entitled 'The Miracle of Mindfulness'

Vivan had been watching me, and when I finished eating, he asked if he should take me home. I said yes, and we took a taxi back to Covent Garden. He was to return to The Oriel, to his friends, and before he left he said to me, 'You have forgotten how to talk to people, how to have fun. Life isn't meant to be a struggle, Diya, you must start living again.' For the first time in our lives, Vivan had spoken to me as if I was an invalid, and I was determined to prove him wrong.

The next day, at 6.30 in the morning, I took the London underground to Bond Street station and walked the rest of the way to Marylebone lane. My nerves were frayed and I arrived one hour before the school opened its doors. I stood outside, studying my schedule: in the morning there was a cooking demonstration of eight dishes including stocks and basic sauces. The students were then expected to reproduce the same items in a two-and-a-half-hour practical in a professional kitchen. In the afternoon, the pastry course followed an almost identical format.

As I read and reread the document in my hand, I began to feel physically sick with fear. Suddenly I heard a voice across the street say, 'Hey, kiddo, it gets better. Everyone is frightened on their first day.' I breathed a sigh of relief, and went over to introduce myself to Ian. He owned the cafe opposite the school and he offered me a cup of chamomile tea to drink while I waited. When it was time for me to go, Ian winked at me and said, 'You'll be fine, kiddo, just use your instinct.'

Ten hours later, I walked out of the school stunned by my fraudulence and fatigue. I had survived a gruelling day in which I swindled my way into reproducing dishes through sheer guesswork. I had not tasted anything.

Ian's words were ringing in my ears as I travelled home on the tube. I knew I was doing myself an injustice and wouldn't be able to get away with it forever. Just as I was about to reach Neal Street, a ten-minute walk from Holborn station where I had disembarked, my stomach began to growl – I realized I hadn't eaten anything the whole day.

For the first time in ten years, I felt genuinely hungry and I was momentarily confused and frightened by the feeling. But I withstood the fear and stopped at Marks and Spencer's supermarket where I purchased a meal of packaged roast chicken with a honey-and-mustard sauce: one of my old favourites.

The house was dark and empty when I entered. Vivan was dining out with his colleagues. I put on all the lights and walked straight up to the kitchen, where I assembled my dinner – roast chicken drizzled with honey mustard sauce, sliced beetroot and cottage cheese.

My fear had abated and I felt excited as I let my hunger guide me. I went up to the patio and ate under a starry sky, enjoying every flavour and texture as if it was my first ever meal. I ate until I felt full. I didn't force myself to finish the food on my plate, such was my delight at being able to feel full. I went to bed that night feeling more alive than I had ever felt before, unable to fall asleep until the early hours of the morning.

For the next one week I continued to cook dishes without tasting them; I misused both my instinct and intelligence. It was inevitable that I would stumble, and when I did, my dignity was brutally sprained and all pretense of accomplishment unsparingly sabotaged.

My undoing – roast chicken with a red wine and herb jus. Like I did every day, I followed the recipe and method with complete precision, but this time I forgot to season the food.

At the end of the cooking session, Chef Francois tasted my dish and gave an incredulous gasp. I looked up at him and saw anger blazing in his eyes.

I stood there shaking, not knowing what I had done, as I watched him butcher the entire chicken and pour a jug full of sauce over it. Then he looked at me and said, 'Eat.' I couldn't move, and loudly he snarled 'EAT!'

The rest of the students began to cower at the manner in which I was being humiliated – in that moment I saw the kindness of human beings, their compassion for my plight visible as I began to eat the food in front of me.

I felt bilious and my stomach churned but I persevered until I finished every morsel of chicken on the plate. Chef Francois hadn't moved from my side and, triumphantly, he said to me, 'Good, now you will never give me such food to eat again.'

I looked away, unable to resist tears, and I began to clean my workspace vigorously as if to disinfect myself of the humiliation.

When I walked out of the school that day, I made my first friend, an American girl named Kathy. She was in my class and had watched my persecution. Without asking me any questions, she said that she too had been an anorexic, that she used to check the incline of her stomach every single day and measure the width between her hip bones to make sure her weight was intact. Then she said to me, 'That's not recovery, you know; this is. You have come this far and you have to trust yourself, your instinct. Tasting food won't kill you, and if you are not hungry at the end of the day, don't eat. You don't have to stick to any formula.'

I was still shaking and she offered to take me out for a drink. I felt unable to go home, to the one inside myself in which I had found solace and safety. So I followed Kathy into a bar and towards the prelude to a relapse.

An hour later, after four large glasses of wine, Kathy had to support me by the arm and help me get into a taxi. She asked me if I was going to be okay and I turned to look at her, but I never did answer.

Once again the house was empty when I arrived. I stumbled up two flights of stairs and collapsed in front of the door to my bathroom. I was high, and I was trying to fight it as I crawled into the bathroom on all fours towards the toilet seat. But I did not have the strength for that fight and shame thrust me forward into a relapse after fifteen months of recovery.

I vomited over and over again, drinking tap water to help flush out the wine, food and humiliation I had endured.

I sat on that bathroom floor for hours, until I heard Vivan come home. Then I dragged myself to bed and I began to whisper the serenity prayer as tears streamed down my face. Finally, I dialled my mother's number. When she answered the phone, I told her I couldn't do it, that I had relapsed. She asked me to come home.

The next morning, I was still awake. I had not been able to sleep. I was haunted by a voice telling me to go to a twelve-step meeting ... Suddenly Vivan burst into my room and said to me, 'You are not quitting. Back yourself, Diya, for once in your life, just back yourself.'

My mother had spoken to him and he had told her in no uncertain terms that she must not allow me to quit. I knew my wish to go home would not be refused if there was a real threat to my recovery ... But I was unsure. So I picked myself up and, unsteadily, I made my way to a twelve-step meeting.

Later that morning, I walked out of the church where the meeting was held, and I never looked back, nor did I attend another addicts anonymous meeting ever again.

In the years since, I have often repeated the following words to myself: 'Back yourself, Diya, just back yourself.'

TWENTY-THREE

'Hi, my name is Diya, and I WAS an addict.'

I don't remember the name of the church at which I attended the twelve-step addicts anonymous meeting – but I do remember being suffused with shame and driven by the need for an escape valve.

Inside the church, I waited impatiently for my turn to speak, my right foot nervously tapping the floor. Finally in an almost incoherent outpouring, I told my fellow addicts what I had done, and I blamed the school for my relapse after a one year and three month period of recovery

The others appeared to agree – they shook their heads as if to tell me my mistake was apparent and that I should not have enrolled in a cooking school.

Relieved by the concurrence, I leaned back against my chair and let myself relax. But as I did, the decision made was gradually dismantled, and once again I had to negotiate the balance beam found on the uneven ground of internal conflict.

At the end of the meeting I was surrounded by voices telling me to not forget that I would never be like other people. They said I could only hope to be an addict in recovery for the rest of my life and that I must keep myself safe. But the loudest voice I heard, the one that could not have been more sure of itself, was the one inside me which screamed, 'No, no, no, this goes against everything you have been fighting for.'

It was the voice of my instinct saying no and I began to listen to it intently … Then, without any residual doubt, I let it guide me out of the door of that church, towards my freedom and my future.

I went straight to the school; I rushed into the locker room to change into my uniform and collect my equipment. I gathered my recipe sheets and went to the kitchen where the practical session was being held. I had missed the cooking demonstration earlier that morning and as soon as Chef Francois caught sight of me, he said in a mocking tone, 'And where have you been, mademoiselle? How do you expect to reproduce this recipe now?'

I responded in a strong and steady voice, 'Chef, I had a problem this morning but I am here now, and since you are my teacher, I expect you to give me the guidance I need.' I looked him straight in the eye when I spoke, a moment I will never forget for the respect I gave myself as I came out of my prison of recovery to face the unknown and unpredictable – to face life.

And I excelled. At the end of the practical, mine was voted the best dish of the day, a reproduction of world renowned chef Paul Bocuse's *Filets de Poissons en Ecailles Croustillantes,* sea bass fillets with crispy potato scales. I had been given a brief summary of how to execute the recipe and, with the use of both my instinct and the instructions,

I produced a dish that satiated all my senses and delivered to me the kind of praise of which I finally felt worthy.

Chef Francois came to me, placed his hands on my shoulders and said that with the kind of drive and determination I had shown, I would travel far and wide. I looked up at him and then straight ahead to where Kathy was standing. She grinned at me and silently mouthed the words, 'Welcome to your recovery, Chef.'

It was a sunny afternoon in the spring of the year 2000 and I decided to walk all the way back to Covent Garden from Marylebone High Street. I was high, so high and it was the kind of high in which the spirit soars when the candle of fear has been exhausted and its flame extinguished.

My senses were alight, and they came alive as I noticed the beautiful scarves in the shop window of Liberty for the very first time, as I breathed in the scent of caramelized peanuts roasting on the sidewalk along Shaftesbury Avenue, as I heard the sweet sounds of a violin being played by a busker near the seven dials of Covent Garden ... And when I tasted my hunger, my spirits soared even higher, bringing a spring to my step as I raced up the stairs of No. 27, Neal Street, Covent Garden.

I knocked on the door of my brother's bedroom and without waiting for an answer I rushed in to tell him I was staying and that I was going to be a chef. He smiled and invited me out to dinner but I declined. I asked him, instead, to dine with me in his home where I would cook a meal.

Before he could respond, I was already on my way to

Marks and Spencer's where, just two weeks earlier, I had stood immobilized by fear.

I walked through the aisles of the food section, appreciating rather than fearing the cornucopia of produce on display: the meat, fish, vegetables, fruit, and so much more that I examined passionately until I made my choice.

I decided to cook a dish I had been taught a few days earlier, a French classic, *Truite aux amandes, beurre noisette,* fillets of trout with flaked almonds in a burnt butter sauce. It was to be accompanied by a simple green salad and some oven-fresh ciabatta, to which I was guided by the aroma emanating from Carluccio's delicatessen, located just opposite Vivan's house.

When I came out of the deli, exhilarated by my purchases, my arms straining against the weight of the groceries, suddenly I stopped …

… And then I smiled as I looked at the front door of No. 27, Neal Street, Covent Garden, London WC2H 9PA, a place I will always remember as the one where I was introduced to myself for the very first time.

> *The time will come*
> *when, with elation*
> *you will greet yourself arriving*
> *at your own door, in your own mirror*
> *and each will smile at the other's welcome,*
> *and say, sit here. Eat.*
> *You will love again the stranger who was your self.*
> *Give wine. Give bread. Give back your heart*

to itself, to the stranger who has loved you
all your life, whom you ignored
for another, who knows you by heart.
Take down the love letters from the bookshelf,
the photographs, the desperate notes,
peel your own image from the mirror.
Sit. Feast on your life.

('Love After Love', by Derek Walcott)

EPILOGUE

I cooked a great meal that night; it was the first one prepared without any succour or subterfuge. I shared it with my brother over a bottle of Pouilly Fuisse, both wine and food powerful in the pleasure they produced – uncompromised by compulsion.

I am a recovered addict and in the years since, I have often eaten too much or very little. Sometimes I drink too much alcohol or I drink just a little – but neither generates the domino effect that defines addiction – I am no longer chained by the label, 'addict'.

In 1762 Jean Jacques Rousseau introduced the social contract with the statement: 'Man is born free and everywhere he is in chains.' It was an observation meant to influence and promote the sovereignty of man as part of society, against autocratic rule.

But now man has become a prisoner of himself. His mind holds sovereign power and it does not reflect the 'general will' of his being.

The social contract must be reinterpreted if man is to

find absolute freedom. The new contract must be between man and himself. In the year 2000, I signed that contract with myself.

I am thirty-nine years old and I never thought I would make it this far. For a long time I never wanted to – but I did, at the end of a long and treacherous road that brought me back to myself, to who I am and to the life that was meant to be mine.

Mine is not the solution. It is an example of a solution that has many faces, faces which appeared when I broke down the definitions that damaged and imprisoned me, when I healed my instinct, restored its virginity and with it the power of all possibility.

The most important dialogue I have ever had, and will continue to have, is the one between me and I.

This book is my practice of step twelve:

'Having had a spiritual awakening as the result of these steps, we tried to carry this message to other addicts, and to practise these principles in all our affairs.'

ACKNOWLEDGEMENTS

To the people who, unknown to them, helped me reach the gates of a new life, no acknowledgement or thanks can ever be enough:

Robert Denning and Dominic Dunne, may you both rest in peace.

Sunil Chakraborty, Nicholas Vreeland and Sanjeev Bhanot … Thank you.

My mother, father and brother: you are, and will always be, my reason to live and celebrate life.